Graeme Bloch

The Toxic Mix

*What's wrong with South Africa's schools
and how to fix it*

TAFELBERG

Tafelberg
an imprint of NB Publishers,
40 Heerengracht, Cape Town
© 2009 (Graeme Bloch)

Cover photo by iStockphoto
Typesetting by Nazli Jacobs
Edited by Roxanne Reid
Indexing by Mary Lennox
Set in Zapf International
Printed and bound by Paarl Print
Oosterland Street, Paarl, South Africa

First edition, first impression 2009

ISBN 978-0-624-04745-2

To Cheryl

Contents

Author's note

We could fill this book with facts and figures. There are plenty to highlight the South African education system's inadequacies. These figures are often included in international comparisons, whether under acronyms like PIRLS or TIMMS or SACMEQ, or by any of the Grade 3 or 6 systemic evaluations for literacy, numeracy and science that the education department has instituted – all of which show that South African children are very far from achieving their full potential.

There are plenty of tables and figures that constitute the evidence on which this book is based. There are details of pass rates, numbers in school, numbers matriculating, teacher training graphs, and so on. Often the evidence is not complete, it is worth saying. There are many statistical gaps in information, and there is no point in hiding this or pretending that we know it all.

Despite these gaps, taken together, using different kinds of angles to confirm the findings, and drawing also on the experience of those in the field, it is still possible to draw quite clear conclusions about why our schools are failing.

There is much qualitative evidence, too, which means that many angles are possible and different stories can be told. There are often both negatives and positives, problems solved and new problems and challenges created or discovered. Stories need to be told, such as of the fantastic amalgamation of fourteen different apartheid education departments into one national department with provincial counterparts. There is the complex story of the reallocation of spend, from richer to poorer schools and between provinces, to begin to redress historical backlogs and inequalities. There is the policy emphasis on fixing the poorer township and rural schools.

We can drill down to specific policies such as the institution of quintiles, or breaking schools down into five groups, based on (surmised) wealth categories of various schools and what this has meant. Fee-free schooling, or maintaining schools that may charge fees, are not simple and one-dimensional choices without consequences and contradictions. For many of the figures, it is up to a point a case of which 'facts' you choose, how you arrange them, and how you decide to tell the story of education. Yet all the stories in these pages attest to the single fact that the vast majority of South African schools are underperforming abysmally.

What follows will rest on sound academic analysis, research and information. It is not my intention to present this in a boring or repetitive way. It is certainly not my intention to be 'academic' in the way that many people unfortunately understand this – up in the air, tendentious, always quoting some authority. I am not trying to prove an academic point or make a controversial point among researchers. Rather, I want to use research and the best of academia to make some clear policy propositions. Conclusions must be based on good information and well-analysed data and evidence.

It is thus my job as author to explore the academic literature and to make sure that this book reflects the latest findings and research. On the one hand, then, I am very conscious of the need to have evidence, facts and figures, and a clear analysis on which to rest the credibility and integrity of the book. On the other hand, it is the book's job to sift through the drama and the debate so that the reader may be presented with clear choices and can clearly decide. Academic research must help us cut through complexity as well as help us confront the unpalatable truths.

While I have read quite widely, there is also a small and particular number of texts on which this book will lean heavily. These texts are partly useful precisely because they themselves summarise many of the debates and the state of consensus in the education field.

The first much-used book will be the UNESCO *Education for All* publication. Secondly, I will draw on a book that I was involved in editing recently. If I say so myself, it is really the only text that puts together concisely and clearly the recent experience of South African education change and education financing choices. *Investment Choices for South African Education* draws on both international experience and the post-apartheid period to give a system-wide analysis of investment options and expenditure choices in education. It provides some of the more up-to-date analysis of problems in education post-apartheid. It points directly to some of the critical reasons for the identified failings.

In the same year that this book came out, the Organisation for Economic Cooperation and Development (OECD) also published a major *Reviews of National Policies for Education in South Africa* that summarises much of the recent evidence on South African education outcomes in particular. It is not necessary always to claim to have done tons of original research. Rather, the OECD report has put together the best findings and figures and helped to arrange them so that we can draw proper conclusions. It seems wasteful and only duplicating unnecessarily to go and redo all the research work that the OECD has gathered, brought together and synthesised so well.

It should also be clear that many arguments will rest on the work of education researchers and policy pioneers who went before. Some of their names are familiar in policy debates in South Africa today. Their rich history of original research and their more academic contributions are not always known and can usefully be acknowledged.

These names include academics such as Linda Chisholm, Jonathan Jansen and Peter Kallaway (all professors), whose bold analysis and consistent critical debate over the years have kept issues of education in the academic and public eye. I obviously borrow heavily from a number of them at different times, but hope I acknowledge them properly where relevant, according to the required conventions. Certainly to borrow can never allow one to plagiarise.

The ideas in this book, and the conceptions of education and where and how it fits into society, are clearly my own. This framework of assumptions will affect the analysis of what has gone wrong in our schools and why. This book is not shy to draw its own clear conclusions, based on its own interpretations of the data and the literature. I am responsible for these choices.

List of abbreviations

ACE	Advanced Certificate in Education
AEM	African Education Movement
AME	African Methodist Episcopal
ANC	African National Congress
ANCYL	ANC Youth League
APLA	Azanian People's Liberation Army
BPA	Black Parents' Association
BPC	Black People's Convention
CATA	Cape African Teachers' Association
CEPD	Centre for Education Policy Development
COSAS	Congress of SA Students
COSATU	Congress of SA Trade Unions
CPSA	Communist Party of South Africa
CSI	Corporate Social Investment
DBSA	Development Bank of Southern Africa
DEC	Department of Education and Culture (Coloured)
DET	Department of Education and Training (African, non-homeland)
DG	Director-general
DOE	Department of Education
EFA	Education for All
FET	Further Education and Training
FOSATU	Federation of South African Trade Unions
GDP	Gross Domestic Product
GEAR	Growth, Employment and Redistribution
HEQC	Higher Education Quality Committee
HOD	Head of Department

HSRC	Human Sciences Research Council
ICT	Information and Communications Technology
ICU	Industrial and Commercial Workers' Union
InSET	In-service Education and Training
IQMS	Integrated Quality Management System
MEC	Member of the Executive Council
MK	Umkhonto weSizwe
MLA	Monitoring Learning Achievement
NAPTOSA	National Professional Teachers' Organisation of South Africa
NCS	National Curriculum Statement
NECC	National Education Crisis Committee
NEEDU	National Education Evaluation Development Unit
NEIMS	National Education Infrastructure Management System
NEPI	National Education Policy Initiative
NGO	Non-Governmental Organisation
NSFAS	National Student Financial Aid Scheme
OBE	Outcomes-based Education
OECD	Organisation for Economic Cooperation and Development
PAAG	Pupils' Awareness and Action Group
PAC	Pan Africanist Congress
PIRLS	Progress in Reading Literacy Study
SACE	SA Council for Educators
SACHED	SA Committee for Higher Education
SACMEQ	Southern and East African Consortium for Monitoring Educational Quality
SADTU	SA Democratic Teachers' Union
SAIRR	SA Institute of Race Relations
SANNC	SA Native National Congress
SAOU	SA Onderwysersunie
SAQA	SA Qualifications Authority
SASM	SA Students' Movement
SASO	SA Student Organisation

SAYCO	SA Youth Congress
SETA	Sector Education and Training Authority
SGB	School Governing Body
SIP	School Improvement Plan
SMT	School Management Team
SRC	Students' Representative Council
TATA	Transvaal African Teachers' Association
TIMMS	Third International Mathematics and Science Study
TLSA	Teachers' League of SA
TRC	Truth and Reconciliation Commission
UCT	University of Cape Town
UDF	United Democratic Front
UN	United Nations
UNESCO	United Nations Educational, Scientific and Cultural Organisation
UNIA	Universal Negro Improvement Association
UNICEF	United Nations Children's Fund
UWC	University of the Western Cape
Wits	University of the Witwatersrand

1 | Facing up to the crisis

South African children are routinely underachieving – not only among the worst in the world, but often among the worst in the southern African region and in Africa as a whole. This is despite vastly superior resources in Africa's most industrialised nation.

There is a great divide between a small minority of schools that are doing OK and the vast majority that are in trouble. Even given the many achievements of post-apartheid democracy, this single sad theme of underperformance will not be hidden by different ways of reflecting on the truth. The stark reality is that some 60–80% of schools today might be called dysfunctional.

There is no shortage of evidence showing how badly the South African education system is performing. International comparisons evaluating literacy, numeracy and science ability clearly show that South African children are not getting it. All the stories in this book confirm the sorry tale of how poorly our education system is performing.

There is no doubt that this is something that needs to be put to rights. Education is the key to growing the skills required in a cut-throat competitive world – the skills to design, plan and implement the changes we need to go forward as a great nation.

Education is about the aspirations and opportunities that young people have. What do they want to make of their lives? Can they think creatively and innovatively about their future in a rapidly changing world? Can they be the best; do they desire to achieve excellence in everything they do?

Education is also about how we live together. What do we know about our fellow South Africans, about their cultures, their needs and aspirations? Do we understand the constitutional imperatives that bind us together? Are our children to be citizens of the world, building peace and solidarity wherever they go? Education is about our common humanity as South Africans in a global world. This is no small thing in a world and a continent beset by recession, endless wars and hatred.

Education helps us, together, to solve the pressing problems of the day, from economic to political and social crises, from global warming to ecological disaster and war.

Education means that as workers at the tip of Africa, where the cradle of civilisation began, we can nonetheless aspire to participate as space scientists contributing to the knowledge of the world or as biotechnologists on the cutting edge of research, inventing new vaccines to combat illness and disease.

It is a tall order that we demand all these things from education. Education has to change society. Like some holy spirit, its influence must reach everywhere to initiate people into the good things that society can offer; education must help us to participate and improve in every field of human and social endeavour.

As if to underline this, UNESCO, in a call around the Education For All Campaign (EFA), had this to say as it, too, planted a bold flag for the benefits of education:

> There is good evidence that the benefits of education to individuals and society are enhanced when its quality is high. For example, better learning outcomes – as represented by pupils' achievement test scores – are closely related to higher earnings in the labour market; thus, differences in quality are likely to indicate differences in individual worker productivity. Furthermore, the wage impact of education quality appears to be stronger for workers in developing countries than for those in more industrialised societies. Empirical research has also demonstrated that good schooling improves national economic potential – the quality of the labour force, again as measured by test scores,

appears to be an important determinant of economic growth, and thus of the ability of governments to alleviate poverty.

Benefits do not arise only from the cognitive development that education brings. It is clear that honesty, reliability, determination, leadership ability and willingness to work within the hierarchies of modern life are all characteristics that society rewards. These skills are, in part, formed and nourished by schools. Similarly, evidence shows that bright but undisciplined male school dropouts who lack persistence and reliability earn less than others with the same levels of ability and cognitive achievement, and will continue to do so beyond school. Schools that encourage the above characteristics more successfully than others will bring greater long-term earnings benefits to the individuals who attend them.

Schools also try to encourage creativity, originality and intolerance of injustice – non-cognitive skills that can help people challenge and transform society's hierarchies rather than accept them. These, too, are important results of good schooling, having broader benefits for society, irrespective of their impact on personal earnings.

Good quality in education also affects other aspects of individual behaviour in ways that bring strong social benefits. It is well known, for example, that the acquisition of literacy and numeracy, especially by women, has an impact upon fertility behaviour. More recently it has become clear that the cognitive skills required to make informed choices about HIV/AIDS risk and behaviour are strongly related to levels of education and literacy. For example, HIV/AIDS incidence in Uganda has fallen substantially in recent years for those with some primary or secondary education, whereas infection rates have remained unchanged for those with no schooling . . . [1]

Education is immensely complex. It has to be, considering all the demands put on a good education.

Look at this in reverse. If education is to affect every aspect of social life, there must surely be an immense number of things in society to which education relates. These in turn will impact on education. Imagine the range of influences and issues that affect the outcomes from the education system, from physical infrastructure and governance to learning time and class size, from learner aptitude to literacy, numeracy and life skills, and from human resources to economic and labour market conditions in the community. UNESCO has identified all these and more.[2] In Chapter 4 I intend to boil down all the areas of influence to three key ones. For the moment, it is enough to acknowledge how complicated it is to get everything right and everything coordinated at the same time.

This book invites South Africans to celebrate the possibilities of a good education. The desire for schools to work is high up on the list of concerns of all South Africans. During the 2009 elections, all parties had education as one of their top three priorities. The famous Polokwane conference of the ANC, which eventually led to the recall of President Mbeki and the ascendancy of Jacob Zuma, put education high on the list of resolutions for a new government to address. There was a series of calls both detailed and general.

Some resolutions called for education to become a central concern of the whole society and a responsibility beyond just the education departments. Another resolution promised to restore the 'noble profession' of teaching, but demanded that teachers be 'in class, on time, teaching' as a quid pro quo.[3] Other resolutions implicitly addressed issues of poverty in education, calling idealistically for fee-free schools and free education to undergraduate level.

There is no shortage of people who want our schools to work. There is a great concern in South Africa that things are going wrong. Even the education department and education authorities reiterate again and again that things are not where they should be.

The call is out to do something about it, before it is too late. Already, thousands of young children have lost the opportunities that a sound education may have opened up. Generation after generation cannot continue to lose access to choices and the possibility of hope and progress.

Who can make a difference?

To do something meaningful about schools, given the deep challenges and extensive underperformance, means that everyone will have to play a role. The ANC at Polokwane was absolutely right to say that education will have to be a broad societal concern, certainly not just a concern of the educationists.

There is a variety of ways to tap the energy, the skills, the experience of citizens in this country. There are things that every single citizen can do, whether it is individuals helping the children of their domestic worker; a community making sure every child in uniform is actually attending school; graduates ploughing back their success by paying someone's way at their old school; or companies contributing hundreds of thousands of Rand through their corporate social investments. More than money, the important thing is the range of skills that can be mobilised and the enthusiasm and energy directed to give every child a chance. Many things can happen very quickly to improve our failing schools.

There are two groups who are going to have to take most of the burden and the strain, who are most responsible for taking the initiative and showing the way to improvement. These are the professionals who make education work and sustain the learning enterprise. Firstly, of course, the government must do its job. From top to toe, from the minister at national level through to the provinces and the officials in every district, the government must be seen to work. Without excuses and unnecessary delays. Government and its officials are there to smooth the way and make the changes happen. They need to serve in a supportive and constructive way, without needless bureaucracy, paperwork and symbolic compliance for its own sake.

The other group who will really need to come on board are the teachers themselves. There are almost 400 000 teachers in our schools. Not every single one can be brilliant, to be sure. There are daily examples of perseverance, of sharing of skills, of long hours and caring support, of teachers who do their jobs with integrity and knowledge. Still, too many teachers get away with not being able to teach; too many engage in antisocial and anti-educational activities, often protected by their unions. Whether teachers are or are not in class, whether they struggle to plan their year and set their agendas, whether they are doing their work well or badly, the public has a right to demand outcomes from teachers. The public needs reassurance that teachers know their trade and their profession and do it well.

Getting teachers right is priority number one if schools are going to work. It will require a mixture of support and laying down the line, an acknowledgment of the complexity of teaching and the many difficulties faced by teachers, alongside a set of demands laying out exactly what is expected of the teachers in our classrooms.

So this book sets out to appeal to all of those citizens who want to make a difference. It calls out for action from citizens who realise that things cannot continue as they are, who understand that they can in fact do something to change it. We all have to act to get things moving, to take responsibility for the challenges our country faces.

This does not mean springing to action without thought, just doing anything and everything that comes to mind all at the same time. It is impossible to fix everything all at once. This book will help to ask what the key drivers are that will have to be chosen. If together citizens really are to make an impact, they will have to find the space and the time to decide and agree on those things that will need to be the points of focus.

The starting point has to be an acknowledgment of what has gone wrong. As anti-apartheid activist, academic and one-time managing director of the World Bank Mamphela Ramphele argues in her book *Laying Ghosts to Rest*,[4] we have to face down the demons and ghosts of the past. Not just what has gone wrong, but what the reasons are, where the causes of the roadblocks and the obstacles are.

This is not a blame game but a determination to identify points of intervention, to understand weaknesses and to decide what has to be fixed to bring the maximum gains. It requires an honest and firm gaze on the shortcomings and a willingness to name the problem.

This book is not a manual. It is not going to help you get your child into a better school. It will not tell you how to deal with discipline problems, or what to do about a headmaster who is not doing his job. It is not going to tell you how to fix a particular problem at the school where your daughter goes, or how to handle a problematic district official. It is not a 'how to' book in that sense of the word. Rather, it helps you to know that these kinds of problems occur right through the system of schooling in South Africa and to understand their impact and implications. Perhaps there is comfort in knowing you are not alone in your worries and concerns. It helps to understand the range of factors that may probably also be contributing to the specific problems that concern you and your child.

This book is written for South Africans who may well have children at school, and therefore certainly have a range of concerns about education. Because of their immediate issues, their minds may have become sharpened to the facts and the challenges. It is human, necessary, legitimate to do the best by your own children, to make sure that they get the most out of their years in the schooling and education system.

Where it all begins

This book is mostly about the school system. As will become clear, schools are not the only places where education happens, where values are passed on and a respect for excellence and achievement is developed. The education system as a whole forms a set of interlocked and interlinking institutions, even 'pipelines': this book could not deal with all the issues and fields of education without getting immensely complicated.

So, here I will concentrate mostly on schooling, more particularly on the primary and secondary schools. There will be some focus on the Further Education and Training (FET) vocational option in the last years of high school. I will obviously look at higher education, particularly whether schools are providing the well-prepared and knowledgeable young students that should be entering the universities, and whether these students are meeting with success. The implications of the school system and its linkages and flows at a number of levels are matters that cannot be sidestepped. We also cannot ignore how failures have a knock-on effect right through the educational pipeline. The entire pipeline and its flows and leakages will have to be addressed.

But this book focuses primarily on a specific band of education and does not touch on other important questions and needs in education, such as adult literacy and 'special needs' education. This is not simply a pragmatic choice. The school system is the solid base on which many other things rest. It is the place where most children find themselves at some stage or another. If we cannot get the schools right, it is unlikely there will be proper fixes in many of the other areas. There is enough going wrong in the schools, enough evidence to get our teeth into, enough dysfunctionality in the school system alone, to get our stomachs churning and our emotions twisted.

For all these reasons, it makes sense to focus mostly on schools, in fact on the public schooling system to be more specific, where more than 96% of children find themselves. With some focus of this kind, we can more carefully explore what the problems are and how we can develop solutions. Are there things we can do, together, to get our schools into shape? We must acknowledge that it is only the starting point of a long and extended journey on the road to a learning nation, but it is an absolutely necessary starting point.

How should we fix our schools? What will make a difference and open access to quality education for all our children? We would surely like the system to work for everyone at the same time as we struggle to build a decent educational path for our own children and in our own homes and schools. This book appeals to this sense of human solidarity and shared concern.

Education is important to the country. This is because schooling does touch on the skills outputs of the nation, whether South Africa will be at the cutting edge and able to compete with nations throughout the globe. Will we have the urge to innovate, the management systems, the ability and capabilities to implement policy plans, to decide what is essential to growing our economy and to ensuring development in South African society?

If we fixed our schools, education could contribute far more to build a shared citizenship, a respect for diversity, a tolerance for each other and for a range of views and customs. All of these are good reasons to worry about how we fix our education system in South Africa. It is a precondition for being sure that we can build a better tomorrow.

Education as it stands today continues to reproduce inequalities in society, inequalities that threaten the stability and comforts of all young people. It is true that these inequalities, and uneven power relations, grow from or originate in divisions and problems in the wider society. These inequalities, the marginalisation and exclusion that is created and reinforced, hold back many from looking ahead to a better shared tomorrow.

Most children find that the education system fails them, penalises them and almost rationalises their ongoing exclusion from the fruits of democracy and change. Education seems to reinforce inequality and shuts children out rather than being inclusive in its aspirations and effect. This is because education is embedded in society, is part of the complex social transitions and inequalities in the first fifteen years of democracy. These in turn were institutionalised well *before* democracy and are a part of what the democratic state inherited.

Education always reflects the wider society; it cannot but be a part of all the problems and achievements of a particular society, whether under colonialism, apartheid or democracy. A divided, greedy, cruel society will never be changed by its education system alone.

Nonetheless, education has its own dynamics too. Above all, its stories and claims of access for all, of the liberating power of knowledge and reason, mean that education will always do more than just reflect society. Education can also change society. Slowly, not always in dramatic ways, knowledge and learning can be a force for change and freedom. This force can be very fundamental and can make an impact on the basic values of a society. Education always carries this contradictory aspect: it conveys the values and concerns of a given society at a point in time, but at the same moment education holds the potential to go further than where we are, to transcend the given and imagine the new.

Identifying the fault lines

Much has been done in the first fifteen years of democracy. There have also been drastic mistakes, such as overambitious curricula, unconsidered teacher retrenchments and the failure to adequately mobilise the enthusiasm and skills base in civil society, to mention only a few.

This book is not about 'getting the balance right' between positive and negative criticism or about a 'balance sheet' assessment between good and bad policies. It is rather about identifying the weaknesses and challenges in the schooling system so that we can work smarter to fix them. It is about understanding the context, being sensitive and sympathetic to the realities and inherited limitations that make education change more difficult than we might wish.

It is also about showing clearly where it is that things are going wrong so that the appropriate interventions can be implemented. It is about focus and drive, about priorities and outcomes, and about the place of each reader in contributing to getting things right. Understanding how the system works, and how it got to where it is, can never take away the fact of human agency as the ultimate determinant of what happens.

The book will approach issues in a systematic way, to take the readers through the arguments and to examine the assumptions as we go along. The context is vital. It is important not to be flip or superficial about problems or to fall back on easy prejudices. There are so many factors at play that it pays to take things slowly, examine them carefully and make sure that all the pieces of the puzzle are in place.

The next chapter will set the scene by looking at the development of black South African education in context. I will look at the history of schooling for blacks in some detail. I will choose selected periods that set the basis for understanding the institutions of educational importance and how they worked. First of all, I will examine education in traditional society, to make the point that African society before colonialism had ways of passing on knowledge, values and skills. These were especially appropriate to the societies of the time and their needs. Formal schooling only came later.

The missionaries were the first to provide education to blacks in a systematic way. Many of the historic schools established by the missionaries are remembered with fondness as centres of excellence and achievement that played a significant role in training the leaders of the liberation struggles to come – schools such as Healdtown (1857), Adams College (1853), Lemana (1906) and Tigerkloof (1904).

But the church contribution has always been ambiguous. On the one hand, missionaries provided modern western (industrial) schooling that helped ensure advance and integration into colonial society at certain levels; on the other hand, the missionaries were also the forerunners of colonialism as it undermined traditional African society. A combination of conquest and new social divisions as capitalism and gold mining transformed South Africa helped put paid to the autonomy of African societies.

Mission schooling was to become a particular target of the Nationalist Party in 1953 as it introduced Bantu Education, which used education specifically as a weapon to ensure a cheap labour force with no rights, and to achieve the goals of segregation in South African society.

The rest of Chapter 2 engages the introduction of apartheid education, its impact, the spread of cheap mass education for blacks, and the fires of resistance that were fanned by these apartheid plans in education. In 1976 the schools exploded in open defiance of segregated education; by 1980 and the mass democratic struggles of the decade, schooling and education struggles were at the centre of resistance as part of the broader forces for change. Teachers, students and parents fought for People's Education under the banner of the National Education Crisis Committee (NECC). This resistance and its achievements are the source of much debate, with some arguing that this was what created the anarchy and instability found in many schools today.

The chapters that follow the historical context leap straight into the contours and challenges of post-apartheid education. How is the education system performing? In Chapter 3 I examine and present evidence to show the many achievements, but also the multiple failures, in education today. This is not just a dry series of education statistics, but an analysis or diagnostic of what is going wrong.

What are the key blockages and failures in the system? How do we organise our understanding of these facts so that we know which key things are causing problems? There is a combination of factors, a toxic mix of causes that come together to keep black education in a state of disrepair. It is a fatal and complex mix of in-class or classroom failings – many related to teachers – combined with poor administration and support around the school, as well as societal factors that together conspire to hold back learners' potential and close down opportunities.

Government and government policy surely cannot escape blame or responsibility for this. Chapter 4 will look at what government has done wrong and how actions and policies have compounded rather than resolved some of the multiplicity of problems. In any case, whatever their intentions and achievements, government programmes are clearly not hitting the ground in a forceful way; there is no critical mass that is driving changes through. Progress is painfully slow and unacceptably incremental. Progress in some areas is often countered by setbacks in others because there is little synergy driving overall towards clearly improved outcomes.

While this book tries to avoid playing the blame game, responsibility still has to be located somewhere. Understanding the context and the causes, being empathetic to the range of difficulties, still does not let officials and teachers off the hook, to be very specific.

Chapter 5 will look at what is being done to address the problems. At many different levels, there are incredible people and programmes that show the way and provide models of what might work. It is amazing to see the many successes and the many people and institutions in education working to make things better. Looking at the good things in education is not meant as an exercise to make us feel better, or to put on rose-tinted Pollyanna glasses. It is to try to find models and approaches that can work.

Chapter 6 suggests how we should build the roadmap ahead, and Chapter 7 tries to propose actions that can be performed by different stakeholders to take us forward. We need a set of practical proposals to help us intervene and contribute to processes of education improvement. We also need a clear national plan and an agreed set of priorities around which to work, so we can slot in our efforts in a loose framework and usefully coordinate ways that maximise results.

Can we fix our ailing, failing schools? Of course we can! In fact, we have to, if South Africa is to take its full place alongside other nations in the world. If we are to keep holding up our heads proudly in the world, we are going to have to be intellectually skilled and academically qualified, confident that our knowledge is global and cutting-edge.

Change will not happen quickly or overnight. Still, there are many things that can be done immediately that would make a difference. Even though there is no quick fix, if we do not start now, with urgency, with unity, we will never achieve anything in the long term either. Without a sense of urgency, our country will surely end in serious trouble, and the loss of our human potential will be unforgivable.

2 | Scars from the past

While we are never victims of the past, we cannot simply shrug off the way the society we inherited has influenced the institutions and the culture of the present. Institutions and attitudes from the past channel the perceptions and shape the possibilities of today.

We can only shake off the negative influences of the past once we become aware of how they have shaped us, so in this chapter I will step back into our history. It is of course not a question of good or bad, but of how things have worked. It is not a case of casting blame or of shirking responsibility, but rather a question of being sensitive to the context and the changing shape of different phases and eras. To this end I wish to go back 400 years or more.

While no one should romanticise traditional society, it is quite clear that traditional societies were well integrated into their environment in South Africa. Societies of hunter-gatherers like the Khoisan and the herders of the Bantu-speaking tribes had sophisticated and developed institutions.

Today the rock paintings of the Western Cape's Cedarberg, the Northern Cape, the Amathole mountains of the Eastern Cape and the Drakensberg in KwaZulu-Natal give evidence of the wide range and spread of the Khoisan people and some insight into their lives. How did they learn their art, where did their common symbols come from, what were the materials and technologies they employed? We have some conjecture and some limited science to give us partial answers to these questions.

White settlers on horseback hunted down the so-called Bushmen (now more correctly called the San people) like vermin, wiping out the last remnants of their bands. In the rural Cape, the Khoi herders were turned into slaves as the fields that sustained their fat-tailed sheep were commandeered by rapidly expanding settlers, using Dutch and then British landownership systems and laws to justify their colonial conquest.

From the start, dispossession and conflict were written into the relations between the white settlers and indigenous inhabitants of the land that became South Africa. Violence and arrogant disregard were branded by fire into the civilising mission of conquest and its repressive façade of order and law. These relations became even more fraught when white settlers clashed with the more powerful autonomous tribes in the Frontier of today's Eastern Cape and the interior of South Africa.

The last of the colonial wars of conquest and dispossession was relatively recent. Chief Bhambatha led the final remnants of his warrior cohorts into the Nkandla forests to carry on their battles of resistance until they were wiped out or led off dispirited to spend their time in the dungeons and prison islands of the British overlords. Bhambatha was finally defeated only in 1906. The British cut off Bhambatha's head; pictures of his head on a stake were used as gruesome but threatening postcards for troops writing home. There must still be people for whom passed-down tales of this resistance are within living if not direct memory.

Not everything in traditional society was idyllic or harmonious. The battle against the elements in a harsh and unforgiving landscape like South Africa's must have been considerable. There was the power of the chief, sometimes used for good, but no doubt often used to build his herds and his lines of patronage over his people. There were gender inequalities held up as tradition. The Difaqane, or wars of dispossession, had swept through southern Africa, destabilising kingdoms throughout the early nineteenth century and laying the basis for divisions that dramatically strengthened the hand of the conquerors. The Nguni-speaking tribes mostly despised the first indigenous people and – like the colonists – also made war on the Khoisan people.

At the same time, there were enormous institutions of pride. All tribes had their *lekgotla*, or council, where traditional democracy held the chiefs and headmen to account and everyone (male) had a voice. The Difaqane, or Mfecane, spearheaded by Shaka saw adaptation of new weaponries and new technologies of war. These had their social base in the *amabutho*, or organisations of young warriors into age formations. Societies inducted and initiated young people into the ways of their elders, from oral traditions to songs to medicines and cosmology.

Overt initiation schools, where circumcised youth learnt the values and mores of their times, or young girls were introduced into the mysteries of their bodies, warned young people of the expectations that society would have of them in their roles and created the social solidarity, age networks and relationships that would sustain them. Annual ceremonies like the reed dance cemented these social relationships and networks and confirmed the place of individual and society in the universe.

Astronomers told tales of the stars and of the origins of the universe; medicine men and women healed the sick and cast the bones to understand the psychological depths and fears of their people. Painting, dance and music flourished, telling the tales of achievement and of the origins of the people in the world, of what had gone before and how the future might be faced.

Plants were used for their nutritional and medicinal qualities, and poisons were mixed to aid the hunt. Animal husbandry flourished as a science; even today Nguni cattle are revered for their style and resilience. The flourishing of agriculture and growth of supplies of wheat and grain to the mines by small-scale peasant farmers in the early 1900s across today's Free State and Lesotho also show the adaptability and skills of the farming techniques used in traditional societies.

While there were no formal schools, the traditions and values of the society, its knowledge, technologies and skills, were passed on, maintained and preserved, and changed.

The overview of traditional society reminds us that learning in society can happen without schools. Independent and autonomous social

DIE PLEK WAAR GOD ONS SEËN

As jy 'n nuusredakteur by 'n TV-kanaal was wat 'n uur lange spesiale program oor die inval in Kanaän moes saamstel, sou jy beslis die mees dramatiese materiaal wat jou filmspan geskiet het, gekies het. Jy sal ongetwyfeld begin met Josua se leër wat deur die Jordaanrivier storm nadat dit op 'n wonderbaarlike manier voor hulle oopgemaak het. Jy sal 'n hele paar minute afstaan aan die week wat hulle rondom Jerigo gemarsjeer het en aan die mure wat donderend ineengestort het. Jy sal dalk die tydelike terugslag by Ai, wat deur sonde onder die volk veroorsaak is, insluit. Maar jy sal sommer gou terugkeer na nog militêre "skok en verbasing" namate meer stede in die hande van die stormende Israeliete val. Jou hoogtepunt sal die toneel wees waar God vir Josua en sy troepe help deur 'n gewelddadige haelstorm oor die vyand te laat losbars – ernstig genoeg om mense te laat sterf – en dan selfs hulle dag te verleng sodat hulle die oorlog kan klaar veg.

Maar sal jy as nuusredakteur hierna kyk na die godsdienstige seremonies by Gilgal? (Jos 4-5). Nee wat! Dit is te oninteressant. TV-kykers soek *aksie*. Laat die spanning voortdurend opbou – moet nooit toelaat dat dit verslap nie. Dís hoe jy kykers boei.

Ek moet bely dat ek self nooit baie aandag aan Gilgal gegee

het nie – totdat ek afgekom het op 'n terloopse verwysing daarna verder met die tydlyn langs, in Rigters 2. Teen dié tyd het Josua reeds gesterf en die Israeliete het vinnig al verder van God af weggedryf. Die eerste sin van hierdie hoofstuk lui: "Die Engel van die Here het van Gilgal af na Bokim toe gegaan."

Waarom sou die Bybel moeite doen om vir ons te vertel *van waar* die Engel van die Here gekom het? Die meeste ander verwysings in die Bybel sê bloot dat God se spesiale Engel by 'n sekere plek verskyn het (soos by Horeb waar die moedelose Elia was, of by die fontein in die woestyn waar Hagar water gedrink het). Die Engel van die Here dra elke keer sy boodskap oor en verdwyn dan weer. Waar die Engel vandaan gekom het, word nie gesê nie.

Maar Gilgal, 'n plekkie 'n kilometer of wat noordoos van Jerigo, het skynbaar die een of ander geestelike betekenis gehad. God was op 'n unieke manier daar teenwoordig. Selfs honderde jare nadat Josua die inval van die land gelei het, het die profeet Samuel herhaaldelik na Gilgal teruggekeer om offers te bring, om vir koning Saul oor sy afvalligheid te konfronteer en om die volk tot hernude toewyding op te roep. Ek glo hierdie gebruik het gespruit uit wat God in Josua se tyd op hierdie plek gedoen het.

Gilgal was die eerste plek waar die Israeliete kamp opgeslaan het nadat hulle die Jordaanrivier oorgesteek het. Dit het hulle "basiskamp" geword, van waar hulle vele militêre invalle onderneem het. Dit was ook 'n opleidingsterrein waar God sy volk drie lesse geleer het, wat toekomstige oorwinnings vir hulle moontlik sou maak. Hierdie drie beginsels is vandag nog vir ons van belang. Hulle vorm saam 'n stel sleutels tot God se blywende teenwoordigheid en seëninge in ons lewe. Ons durf nie die Israeliete se verhaal verder lees sonder dat ons na die drie lesse van Gilgal gekyk het nie.

1. Kyk terug voordat jy verder gaan

By Gilgal het Josua God se opdrag uitgevoer toe hy twaalf groot klippe geneem het uit die Jordaanrivier – wat God op 'n wonderbaarlike manier laat opdam het sodat sy volk daardeur kon stap – en dit toe as gedenktekens opgerig het. Die doel van hierdie klippe was om gesprekke met die volgende geslagte aan te wakker: "Wanneer julle kinders julle eendag vra: 'Wat beteken hierdie klippe vir u?' moet julle vir hulle sê die Jordaan se water is voor die verbondsark van die Here afgesny" (Jos 4:6-7). Só sou die wonder van God se krag en voorsiening weer en weer bevestig word.

Hierdie klippe was nie afgode wat aanbid moes word nie. Hulle was eerder 'n getuienis van die trou van die enigste ware God. Hulle het aan die volk rede gegee om God te prys. En in só 'n atmosfeer het "die Engel van die Here" heeltemal tuis gevoel.

> Dit sal help om nie te fokus op die probleme wat voor ons opgestapel staan nie. Ons moet eerder feesvier oor die God wat reeds sy krag en voorsiening in ons verlede geopenbaar het.

Wanneer die volk Israel ook al getuur het na die grense van hulle kamp, het hulle vir seker gewonder hoeveel Kanaänitiese leërs in die skaduwees of agter mure skuil, wagtend om hulle aan te val. Maar wanneer hulle hulle oë op die twaalf klippe gerig het, het hulle vrese verdamp. Hulle God het so pas die Jordaanrivier, wat in vloed was, laat opdam sodat hulle daardeur kon trek! Natuurlik sal Hy ook die pyle en klippe van die vyand kan keer.

Wanneer ons vandag voor struikelblokke en opponente te staan kom, sal dit help om nie te fokus op die probleme wat voor ons opgestapel staan nie. Ons moet eerder feesvier oor die God wat reeds sy krag en voorsiening in ons verlede geopenbaar het. Ons hoef nie besorg of angstig te wees nie. Ons behoort ons lewe en gedagtes te anker in God se verbysterende prestasies van die verlede.

Die Bybel sê: "Nader tot God en Hy sal tot julle nader" (Jak 4:8). Skynbaar leef alle Christene nie ewe naby aan God nie. Al behoort ons almal aan sy familie, leef sommige nader aan sy dinamiese krag as ander. Wanneer ons lewe gevul is met lofprysing en dankbaarheid oor die genade wat in die verlede aan ons betoon is, ervaar ons dat God in die hede nog nader aan ons kom.

Psalm 22:4 sê oor God: "U is tog die Heilige wat woon waar die lofsange van Israel weerklink!" Wat 'n verskil sal dit maak as ons een keer per uur sou gaan stilstaan en sê: "Ek prys U, Here! U was so goed vir my! Ek sê vir U dankie." Dink net hoeveel meer vreugde en vrede ons die hele dag lank sal ervaar.

Dit sal nie net waardevol wees op die sonskyndae nie, maar veral in tye waarin ons beproef word of verlies ervaar. Natuurlik kom probleme ons lewe lank oor ons pad. Dit is onvermydelik. Maar in plaas daarvan om bekommerd te wees, kan ons ons probleme hanteer in die lig van alles wat God in die verlede vir ons gedoen het. Toe ons met ons rug teen die muur gestaan het, het God 'n deur van voorsiening oopgemaak. Hy is vandag nog dieselfde God.

George Müller het in die 1800's 'n kinderhuis in Bristol, Engeland, bestuur. Meer as 100 000 kinders is in 'n tydperk van 50 jaar daar versorg. Hy het gesê God het hom beveel om nie geld vir hierdie werk in te samel nie. Hy moes net vertrou en wag. As gevolg hiervan het sy geloof en gebedslewe dramaties gegroei. Een Oujaarsaand, toe hy 59 jaar oud was, het hy in 'n preek gesê:

"Deur die goedheid van die Here word ons toegelaat om nog 'n jaar binne te gaan – en die gedagtes van baie onder ons is ongetwyfeld vol toekomsplanne en gevul met die verskillende vrese wat ons werk en diens aan die Here meebring … Sorg egter in die eerste plek dat julle *bly is in die Here.* Ander sake kan jou aandag opeis, die werk van die Here kan selfs dringend aandag van jou verg, maar ek herhaal doelbewus: Dit is van deurslaggewende en die uiterste belang dat julle daarna sal streef *om bly te wees in God.* Streef elke dag daarna om dit die belangrikste prioriteit in julle lewe te maak. Dit was my vaste en aanvaarde voorneme in die afgelope 35 jaar."[2]

Om "bly te wees in die Here" in die lig van sy trou tot vandag toe – dit is die eerste les wat Gilgal ons leer. Natuurlik sal ons voor uitdagings te staan kom, maar laat ons dit nie ons hooffokus maak nie. Laat ons eerder kies om dankbaar te wees vir die seëninge wat God reeds in ons lewe uitgegiet het. Die Een wat ons uit "Egipte" gelei het, wat ons sonde vergewe en ons sy eiendom gemaak het, sal ons nie nou in die steek laat nie.

Kommer verander immers niks nie. God wil hê ons moet eerder na die twaalf klippe in ons lewe kyk. Elke Christen het beslis minstens 12 gedenkstene aan God se goedheid in die verlede toe ons Hom regtig nodig gehad het. Sommige van ons het 12 000!

Elke Christen het beslis minstens 12 gedenkstene aan God se goedheid in die verlede. Sommige van ons het 12 000!

Ek het 'n hele versameling lofprysingsgedenkstene in my lewe weens die manier waarop God ons kerk na die huidige gebou in Smithstraat gebring het. Ná alles wat ons in die afgelope paar jaar moes deurmaak, sal jy my nooit kan oortuig dat ons God nie die God is wat wonderbaarlik kan voorsien nie. Ons kon skaars in die vorige gebou in Flatbushweg pas. Ons het elke Sondag drie dienste gehou in 'n teater wat in 'n ouditorium omskep is en sitplek vir slegs 1 200 mense gehad het. Mense moes in aangrensende vertrekke sit en die diens op TV-skerms volg. Ons kinders en jongmense het ingedruk gesit in keldervertrekke wat gans te klein was.

Een Sondagmiddag in 1996, toe ek by die kerkgebou aangekom het vir die halfvierdiens, was daar 'n vrou wat haar kind by die kinderkerk wou laat aansluit. Ek het gehoor hoe die werker vir haar sê: "Dit spyt my, maar ons is heeltemal vol. Daar is geen plek vir jou seun nie." Ek het gesien hoe daardie ma se skouers val. Sy sou haar seun saam met haar moes neem. Hy sou saam met haar in die voorportaal moes sit en die diens op 'n TV-skerm moes volg. As hy rusteloos sou word, sou sy 'n deel van die boodskap misloop – en intussen sou die seun die kans verbeur om meer van Jesus te leer op 'n manier wat by sy ouderdom pas. Ek het baie hartseer gevoel. Deur die hele middagdiens heen kon ek daardie vrou en haar seun nie uit my gedagtes kry nie.

"Here, dit behoort nie te gebeur nie," het ek gebid. "Dit is die huis van die Here. Iemand wat twee verskillende treine moet haal om hier uit te kom, moet die geleentheid hê om U ongehinderd te aanbid, en haar kind moet hier onderrig en liefde ontvang. Wat gaan ons hieraan doen?"

In daardie selfde week nog het ek en die ander leraars bymekaargekom en ek het vir hulle beskryf wat ek gesien het. Ons het begin bid: "God, dit kan nie u wil wees dat mense hier weggewys word nie. Wat beplan U vir ons?" Ons het 'n paar dae lank die wil van die Here gesoek. Ons het tot die gevolgtrekking gekom dat, al het God ons ryklik in daardie gebou geseën, ons tyd daar verby was. Sy toekoms het iets méér vir ons ingehou. Wat kon dit wees?

Ons het nie geweet nie. Wat ons wel besef het, was dat iets onmiddellik sou moes verander, selfs al was dit net tydelik. Totdat ons 'n ruimer gebou kon bekom, het die leiers besluit om 'n ekstra diens te hou. Ons sou elke Sondag om nege-uur, twaalfuur, drie-uur én sesuur 'n diens hê. Met elke diens wat tot twee uur kon duur, sou dit beslis 'n marathondag wees. Maar ons sou enigiets 'n paar jaar lank kon volhou, het ons vir onsself gesê.

Min het ons geweet dat dit sés jaar sou duur voordat ons die "Beloofde Land sou binnegaan". Ons het aan baie deure geklop en in baie doodloopstrate beland voordat God ons uiteindelik na die historiese Loew's Metropolitan Theater gelei het. Hierdie gebou was in die hartjie van Manhattan se middestad en het 'n glorieryke geskiedenis gehad, maar dit was in daardie stadium verskriklik vervalle. Water het die eens pragtige neoklassieke plafon beskadig. Die waterpype, verhittingstelsel en elektriese bedrading was 'n resep vir 'n ramp. Daklose alkoholiste en dwelmverslaafdes het dit as skuiling gebruik. Party van die rotte daar was so groot dat hulle net sowel met 'n aktetas in die hand en die *New York Times* onder die een arm ingedruk daar kon rondskarrel!

Ja, daar kon 4 100 mense inpas toe dit in 1918 gebou is. Dit was destyds die grootste teater in Noord-Amerika. Buiten die ouditorium was daar ook drie aangrensende kantoorgeboue. Die kompleks het oneindige potensiaal gehad. En die ligging was uitstekend omdat veelvuldige moltrein- en busroetes daar by-mekaarkom. Al wat ons nodig gehad het, was geld – baie geld.

Maar ons het geen geld gehad nie. Ons is nie 'n ryk, voorstedelike gemeente nie. Ons het 'n middestadgemeente waaraan vele loon-werkers, studente, enkelouers en 'n hele klompie werklose mense behoort. Ek het van beter geweet as om groot skenkings van die gemeentelede te vra. Daarom het ek besluit om 'n maandelikse dankoffer vir hierdie projek in te samel. Ek het die gemeente gevra om dit te oorweeg om elkeen $50 te skenk. Die res van die geld, het ek besef, sou van elders moes kom.

In daardie tyd het *The 700 Club* my genooi vir 'n onderhoud oor my eerste boek, *Fresh Wind, Fresh Fire*. Die gasheer, Pat Robertson, het my gevra hoe dit met die kerk gaan. Ek het vir hom van ons omstandighede vertel, en hy het gesê dat hy graag op 'n manier sou wou help. Die volgende week was ek geskok toe ek 'n brief van hom ontvang waarin hy $1 miljoen aan ons belowe het! Ek het hom nie eens direk vir geld gevra nie.

Ons het hierdie gebeurtenis as 'n "gedenksteen" beskou – 'n voorsiening van God wat ons aangemoedig het om voort te gaan met ons droom. Ons geloof het gegroei. Ons het die eienaars van die Loew's Metropolitan Theater genader met 'n dapper aanbod van $6,3 miljoen – kontant. Hulle het dit aanvaar.

Sommer gou het God die res van hierdie bedrag voorsien, en die eiendom het aan ons behoort. Ons was oorstelp van vreugde. Ons het gedink ons geloofsreis was voltooi. Maar dit was voordat ons die koste van die restourasiewerk begin bereken het!

Ons het gou besef dat, omdat dit New York was, ons vakbond-werkers vir alles sou moes gebruik. Elektrisiëns het destyds by-voorbeeld $90 per uur verdien. En dit was besonder ontstellend om oor die bouterrein te stap en te sien hoe sommige van hulle tydens werkure dagga rook. In 'n stadium is daar van ons vereis om 'n ekstra werker in diens te neem, wat volgens ons volkome onnodig was. Maar ons het geen keuse gehad nie. Die vakbonde het die mag gehad om die hele projek te eniger tyd te kelder. Hulle het ook 'n dreigende waarskuwing gerig oor vreemde "ongelukke" wat in die middel van die nag in die gebou sou kon gebeur.

Ek onthou dat ons finansiële bestuurder my eenkeer ingelig het dat ons nog $600 000 binne 48 uur nodig gehad het, anders sou die werk stopgesit word. My vrou, Carol, was daardie dag nie by die huis nie. Sy het haar ma, wat in daardie tyd siek was, gaan versorg. Die Here het my daardie oggend oortuig om nie soos gewoonlik kantoor toe te gaan nie, maar om eerder om sy hulp te smeek in 'n gebedskamertjie wat ons op ons solder ingerig het.

Ek het in daardie solderkamer gebly van tienuur die oggend tot halfses die middag. Die hele tyd het ek tot God geroep om Hom as ons magtige Voorsiener te openbaar. In daardie ure het ons 'n hele paar telefoonoproepe en boodskappe ontvang – en die geld wat mense geskenk het, was genoeg om in daardie week se behoeftes te voorsien.

Dit was nie die enigste keer dat God op die nippertjie vir ons voorsien het nie. Eenkeer moes ons binne twee weke $1,4 miljoen in die hande kry. Die Here het tot ons hulp gekom. 'n Ander keer het ons $6 miljoen nodig gehad om die eerste fase van die restourasiewerk te voltooi. Ek het teruggekom van 'n sendingreis in Suid-Amerika en die stapel pos wat opgehoop het terwyl ek weg was, begin oopmaak. Binne die eerste tien minute het ek 'n koevert oopgemaak waarin 'n belofte van $1 miljoen was – en nog een van $5 miljoen! Ek het glad nie verwag dat ons sulke skenkings sou ontvang nie.

In Maart 2002 het ons by ons nuwe gebou ingetrek, en toe weer "slegs" drie dienste per Sondag gehou omdat daar meer mense in die gebou kon pas. Dit was op die ou end 'n ongelooflike aanbiddingsplek vir ons bediening. Ons sou ons nooit kon indink watter seëninge God daar vir ons sou gee nie. Elke keer wanneer ek by daardie gebou instap, kyk ek op na die pragtig plafonne wat herstel is, of ek hoor hoe die lugreëling aangeskakel word – en dan word ek herinner aan hoe getrou God is. Wat 'n ongelooflike gedenksteen het Hy vir ons voorsien!

Nog meer merkwaardig is dat die waarde van die eiendom die hoogte ingeskiet het ná die tragedie van 9/11. Op daardie afgryslike dag het New York honderdduisende vierkante meter se kantoorruimte verloor. Vele maatskappye het sedertdien die middestad van Brooklyn begin oorweeg as die plek waarheen hulle hulle kantore wou verskuif. 'n Tyd daarna het 'n vooraanstaande ontwikkelaar, Bruce Ratner, toe die New Jersey Nets, 'n professionele basketbalspan, gekoop

> Buitestanders het soms gemeen: "Julle mense moet slim wees met beleggings in die eiendomsmark. Julle het net op die regte oomblik gekoop." Nee, ons het geen benul gehad wat ons doen nie.

en besluit om vir hulle 'n nuwe tuiste in Brooklyn te bou. Hierdie nuwe kompleks, die Atlantic Yards – wat net ses blokke van ons kerk af geleë is – sluit in 'n sportstadion met 18 000 sitplekke plus twee yslike kantoorgeboue, deeltitelwooneenhede en ruimte vir ander handelsondernemings, wat altesaam ongeveer $4,1 *miljard* werd is. Dit alles het die waarde van eiendom in die omgewing skerp laat styg.

As ons hierdie kerkgebou iewers van die grond af moes opbou, sou ons teen 'n astronomiese bedrag nog 'n hele blok moes koop om genoeg parkering te kon voorsien. Maar omdat die gebou voorheen 'n teater was – 'n plek waar die publiek bymekaargekom het – was dit nie nodig dat ons aan hierdie regulasie moes voldoen nie. Ons het in elk geval nie veel parkeerruimte nodig nie, want meer as die helfte van die lidmate van ons kerk maak van openbare vervoer gebruik.

Buitestanders het soms gemeen: "Julle mense moet slim wees met beleggings in die eiendomsmark. Julle het net op die regte oomblik gekoop." Nee, ons het geen benul gehad wat ons doen nie. Al wat ons geweet het, was dat God wou hê ons moes meer ruimte hê om sy werk te kon doen, en Hy sou getrou wees om dit vir ons moontlik te maak. En Hy was beslis getrou!

Ek verwag nie dat ek ooit weer in my lewe so 'n groot bouprojek sal aanpak nie. Maar ek is seker daar sal ander uitdagings opduik. Wanneer dit gebeur, sal ek terugkyk na die stapel "gedenkstene" wat ons om ons opgerig het. En ek sal sê: "Onthou julle hoe God in die verlede in ons groot behoeftes voorsien het? Hy sal dit weer doen. Hy is die God wat vir sy kinders voorsien."

As ons vergeet van die oorwinnings in die verlede, swig ons voor 'n soort geestelike geheueverlies. Dit is veel beter om die oorweldigende vrees en angs te oorwin met 'n vreugdevolle, positiewe en dankbare gesindheid. Wanneer ons God se goedheid onthou en vier, sien ons reeds die volgende seëning wat om die hoek begin verskyn. En ons beweeg vol selfvertroue vorentoe.

2. Moenie in ongehoorsaamheid verder gaan nie

Die tweede les van Gilgal vind ons in Josua 5. Die geslag wat uit Egipte gekom het, het iets langs die pad vergeet. In die 40 jaar wat hulle in die woestyn rondgeswerf het, het hulle opgehou om die teken van die verbond wat God met Abraham, Isak en Jakob gesluit het te onderhou. Hierdie teken was besnydenis. As jy 'n manlike Hebreër was, is jy besny. Maar terwyl God se volk in die woestyn rondgeswerf het, het hulle sy verbondsbepalings verwaarloos wanneer daar ook al 'n seun gebore is. Daarom het God wesenlik vir hulle gesê: "Staak alles. Die huidige geslag leef in ongehoorsaamheid. Moet nie 'n tree verder gee voordat julle hierdie saak opgelos het nie."

Toe begin Josua in die daaropvolgende paar dae met 'n yslike besnydenisprogram. Toe hulle klaar was, het die Here gesê: "Vandag het Ek julle bevry van die smaad wat van Egipte se tyd af op julle rus" (Jos 5:9). Die Ou Afrikaanse Vertaling sê: "Vandag het Ek die smaad van Egipte van julle afgewentel." Dit is inderdaad hoe daardie plek sy naam gekry het: "Gilgal" klink soos die Hebreeuse woord vir "rol" of "wegrol". Gilgal was die plek waar die Israeliete weer in ooreenstemming "gerol" of "gewentel" het met God se bepalings sodat Hy hulle kon seën in die oorloë wat voorgelê het.

Vandag praat ons nie dikwels oor hierdie verband tussen gehoorsaamheid en God se seën nie. Ons verkies om te sê God is liefde en ons is Christene; daarom beroep ons ons bloot op die beloftes van sy getrouheid, ongeag hoe ons leef. Ons verwag dat God ons sal seën, selfs al is ons oneerlik by die werk of al is ons hart vol bitterheid. Ons dink nie eens daaraan dat God sy goedheid van ons sal weerhou omdat ons só leef nie. Niemand is tog volmaak nie, of hoe?

Ek sê nie God sal weier om ons te help of om deur ons te werk tensy ons sonder sonde is nie. Nie een van ons is immers volkome sondeloos nie. Maar daar is 'n groot verskil tussen iemand wat waarlik soos Christus wil leef maar soms tekortskiet, en iemand wat voortdurend die bepalings in die Bybel verontagsaam. As laasgenoemde in 'n krisis sou uitroep: "O God, o God, help my asseblief!" is dit skynheilig.

God het my al meer as een keer oortuig dat daar 'n vorm van ongehoorsaamheid in my lewe is, soos 'n gesindheid wat ek openbaar. Ek en Carol het al dikwels in die verlede 'n hele paar Sondagoggende "meningsverskille" gehad op pad kerk toe. Maar sodra die eerste diens begin, staan ek daar en sing saam met die gemeente en ek hoor hoe Carol die klawerbord speel, en dan besef ek eenvoudig ek durf nie opstaan en die aankondigings lees nie, wat nog te sê preek. Ek staan dan eerder op, stap na waar die musiekgroep is en fluister in haar oor: "Ek is jammer oor wat ek vanoggend gesê het." En sy knik haar kop in vergifnis terwyl sy verder speel.

By ander geleenthede lees ek dalk die Bybel in my stiltetyd en dan lê God die vinger op my ongehoorsaamheid en sê vir my: "Jy moet dit laat staan." Wanneer dit ook al gebeur, kan ek dit nie eenvoudig ignoreer nie. Ek moet dit waarop God my aandag gevestig het, uit my lewe verwyder.

God vra van sy kinders om in die lig te lewe "soos Hy in die lig is" (1 Joh 1:7). Weer eens is dit nie gelykstaande aan 'n sondelose lewe nie. Maar dit beteken wel dat ons bereid sal wees om deursigtig en opreg te wees. Dit beteken ook ons sal berou toon wanneer God ons op ons ongehoorsaamheid wys, net soos Hy dit met die volk by Gilgal gedoen het. As ons kies om in die sonde te volhard het ons geen waarborg dat God ons sal seën nie. Hy is nie ons marionet nie. Sy genade gee nie aan ons toestemming om te leef net soos ons wil nie. Hy verwag van ons toewyding en gehoorsaamheid aan sy Woord.

Ek het eenkeer tydens 'n gebedskonferensie in 'n staat in die weste van die land hieroor gepraat. Toe ek by hierdie punt in die Israeliete se verhaal kom, het ek gesê: "Alles het tot stilstand gekom voordat die Israeliete vir die oorlog teen Jerigo kon optrek, want God het gesê: 'Nee, julle mag nie gaan nie. Die geslag wat uit Egipte gekom het, is nie besny nie.' Dit was die teken wat God vir Abraham gegee het. Dit het hom en sy familie as God se eiendom gemerk.

"Net so kan ons nie wetend in ongehoorsaamheid leef en verwag dat God ons sal help en seën nie. As Hy dit sou doen, sou Hy ons aanmoedig om opstandig te wees. Ons kan nie vir God in ons lewe hê en terselfdertyd vasklou aan die sonde waarvoor Hy sy Seun laat sterf het nie."

Die boodskap was duidelik genoeg om te verstaan. Maar op daardie oomblik het ek aangevoel dat ek die gehoor heeltemal verloor het. 'n Muur het tussen ons verrys – 'n muur van misverstand, het ek sommer aangeneem. Die mense het net na my gestaar. Die entoesiasme wat hulle tien minute vroeër getoon het, was skoonveld.

Ag nee, het ek vir myself gesê. Die kommunikasie tussen ons is nou verbreek. Hulle volg my nie meer nie. Dalk het ek dit nie heeltemal reg vir hulle verduidelik nie en nou is hulle verward. Daarom het ek in my hart gefluister: "Here, help my om dit beter te verduidelik. Hulle verstaan nie die boodskap nie. Ek het my nie goed van my taak gekwyt nie."

Ek het dieselfde argument weer verduidelik. En ek het Psalm 66:18 aangehaal: "As daar sonde in my hart was, *sou die Here nie geluister het nie.*" Dit was immers 'n gebedskonferensie. Ons wou tog in die eerste plek hê dat die Here na ons sal luister, nie waar nie?

Hoe meer ek gepraat het, hoe meer het die gehoor verstar. En toe het ek iets begin besef. Dit was nie 'n muur van misverstand nie. Dit was 'n muur van verwerping. Hierdie gehoor wou nie hoor dat 'n mens iets moet prysgee of iets in jou lewe moet aanpas om gehoorsaam te wees aan God se wil nie.

Ek het oor my woorde begin stotter. Hulle wou hoor dat Jesus hulle tegemoet sou kom, waar hulle ook al is – en hulle net só sou laat voortleef. Hy moes nie probeer om hulle anders te laat leef nie. Hulle wou vir Jesus in hulle lewe hê, maar op hulle voorwaardes.

Ek het teruggedeins. "Here, gebeur dit regtig waar?" het ek saggies gebid. "Dit voel of ek nou hier in 'n stryd gewikkel is."

> Hoe meer ek gepraat het, hoe meer het die gehoor verstar. En toe het ek iets begin besef. Dit was nie 'n muur van misverstand nie. Dit was 'n muur van verwerping.

Toe het ek weer vorentoe geleun en gesê: "Miskien dink sommige van julle julle kan maar in sonde bly leef, julle kan maar jok by die werk, julle kan maar rondslaap – en steeds maar net op 'n knoppie druk om 'n 'kits-God' te kry. Dit werk nie só nie.

"As julle dink ek het al die pad van die stad New York af hierheen gekom sodat julle vir my kan hande klap en ek vir julle kan sê wat julle wil hoor, luister julle vanaand na die verkeerde spreker. Wat julle ook al van my dink, ek moet vir julle die waarheid vertel, ander sal ek God klaaglik in die steek laat."

Dit was doodstil in die vertrek. Niemand het eens "amen" gesê nie. Niemand het íets gesê nie.

"Julle kan nie sonde doen en terselfdertyd God se seën ontvang nie. Dit is wat Gilgal beteken. Die Israeliete kon dalk gesê het: 'Ja, maar ons is die kinders van Abraham, Isak en Jakob.' Biologies was dit waar – maar hulle vertikale verhouding met God was in 'n krisis." Ek het hierdie boodskap weer en weer onderstreep. "Begryp julle dit? Verstaan julle wat ek sê?"

Weer het ek gehuiwer. Daar was niks nie, net die stilte. Almal het ongemaklik gevoel. Ook ek.

Skielik het 'n man van agter in die ouditorium uitgeroep: "Moenie ophou praat nie! Moenie bang wees nie! Jy is reg – ons moet dit hoor!" Die dreigende trane het sy stem hees gemaak. "Gaan voort! Sê dit!"

Dit was al wat ek nodig gehad het om my volstoom te laat voortgaan. Ek het met mag en mening die boodskap herhaal. Eers toe het dit vir my begin voel die gehoor reageer op my woorde.

Toe het ek na die laaste punt van my boodskap aanbeweeg – die Israeliete wat die paasfees by Gilgal gevier het (Jos 5:10-12) – het ek 1 Johannes 1:9 aangehaal: "Maar as ons ons sondes bely – Hy is getrou en regverdig, Hy vergewe ons ons sondes en reinig ons van alle ongeregtigheid."

Ek het gesê: "God wil nie julle pret bederf nie. Hy weet net sommige dinge wat ons naderlok, kan ons vernietig. My dogter Susie het as dogtertjie deur 'n fase gegaan waarin sy dol was oor vuurhoutjies en messe. Ek moes ingryp en sê: 'Nee!'

"Julle reinste dae sal julle gelukkigste dae wees. Die Israeliete het hulle verhouding met God by Gilgal herstel, en só is hulle voorberei om verder te trek en die land te gaan verower."

Ná my boodskap by daardie konferensie het ek na my hotel-kamer toe teruggegaan. Ek het gesien my hemp was sopnat gesweet, asof ek in 'n vuisgeveg betrokke was. Ek het geworstel met verbystering en wanhoop.

Die volgende oggend vroeg het 'n bestuurder my kom oplaai om my lughawe toe te neem sodat ek my vlug huis toe kon haal. Op pad lughawe toe het ek 'n Target-winkel raakgesien. "Kan ons net gou hier stilhou sodat ek iets kan koop om vir my kleinseun saam te neem?" het ek gevra. Hy het op die parkeerterrein gaan stilhou.

Ek het in een van die gangetjies af geloop op soek na iets waarvan 'n agtjarige seun sou hou toe 'n man van in die twintig vanuit die teenoorgestelde rigting na my toe aangestap kom. Skielik het hy uitgeroep: "Jim Cymbala!"

Ek het gaan staan. "Ja?" het ek geantwoord.

"Haai! Ek was gisteraand daar toe jy met ons gepraat het."

"O."

"Dit was regtig 'n kragtige boodskap," het hy gesê. "Wat jy oor Gilgal gesê het, het regtig tot my ma deurgedring."

"Ja?" het ek gesê, nuuskierig om meer te hoor.

"Sy was daar, en sy is 'n gelowige. Ná die tyd het sy my iets interessants vertel – jou boodskap het haar so geraak dat sy gaan bid vir 'n manier om die vriend saam met wie sy nou bly, te verlaat."

"Wát?" Ek kon nie glo wat ek so pas gehoor het nie.

Hy het sy woorde herhaal. "Sy en hierdie man woon saam. En sy gaan nou begin bid dat sy die krag sal kry om daar uit te trek."

Ek het die jong man aan sy arm gegryp. "Meneer," het ek volkome ernstig vir hom gesê, "ek wil hê jy moet iets gaan doen die oomblik dat jy by hierdie winkel uitstap. Ek wil hê jy moet jou ma bel, vir haar sê jy het my toevallig raakgeloop en dan hierdie boodskap van my af aan haar oordra: 'Moenie oor hierdie saak bid nie. Dit sal oneerbiedig teenoor God wees. Trek net uit! Jy hoef oor niks te bid wat God reeds sonde genoem het nie.'"

Hy het verbaas na my gekyk. "Goed, ek sal haar sê," het hy geantwoord en duidelik gehoop dat ek sy arm sou laat los.

Ek het by die winkel uitgestap nadat ek 'n sweetpaktop vir

my kleinseun gekoop het. Terwyl ek na die wagtende motor toe teruggestap het, het ek my die hele tyd afgevra hoe wyd hierdie uiters vreemde gesindheid al onder kerkgangers in ons land en in die wêreld versprei het.

Ander leraars het al vir my gesê dat hierdie denkpatroon deesdae glad nie ongewoon is onder mense nie. Sommige TV-predikers vererger inderdaad die probleem deur hulle gebruik om die woord *sonde* tot elke prys te vermy. Hoekom doen hulle dit? vra jy dalk. Omdat die kyksyfer-ghoeroes vir hulle sê kykers skakel dadelik oor na 'n ander kanaal wanneer jy vir hulle sê hulle moet ophou om iets te doen. Hulle wil dit nie hoor nie.

Nie lank gelede nie het twee Joodse sakemanne, 'n pa en seun, hier in Brooklyn in my kantoor gesit en 'n eiendomstransaksie bespreek. Hulle albei is goeie mense en baie suksesvol in die sake-wêreld. Omdat hulle met 'n Christenleraar gesels het, het hulle vir my vertel hoe graag hulle albei na 'n sekere gewilde TV-prediker luister.

"Hoe so?" het ek gevra.

"Hy is so goed! Jy weet, in ons lewe fokus ons op twee dinge: geld en familie. Dit is al waarvoor ons leef. En hierdie prediker praat gereeld oor hoe jy vir jou familie kan versorg. Hy sê ook jy kan sekere beginsels uit die boek van Spreuke volg en baie geld maak. Hy sê alles wat vir ons belangrik is."

My moed het in my skoene gesak toe ek dink aan 'n enorme gehoor wat byna nooit die boodskap van die apostel Paulus hoor nie: "Ek het sowel die Jode as die Grieke ernstig vermaan om hulle tot God te bekeer en in ons Here Jesus te glo" (Hand 20:21). Vergelyk dit met die standpunt wat deesdae verkondig word: "Moenie vir mense sê hulle doen iets verkeerds nie. As jy dit doen, sal hulle dalk wegstap. En om mense aanstoot te gee kan nooit geregverdig word nie."

Ons Heiland het nie stilgebly nie. Johannes 6 vertel vir ons van 'n keer toe Jesus gepraat en die mense besluit het om Hom nie meer te volg nie. Maar Hy het nie agter hulle aangehardloop en gesê nie: "Wel, mense, dalk kan Ek dit so 'n bietjie verander. Ek is jammer – het dit julle aanstoot gegee? Ek het seker my konsentrasie 'n oomblik verloor. Kom Ek stel alles weer vir julle reg."

Gilgal sê vir ons ons moet berou toon wanneer ons sonde gedoen het. Ons moet ons wil aan God se wil en sy planne ondergeskik stel. Ons moet Hom alle rede gee om vir ons te glimlag en 'n kanaal oop te maak waardeur Hy ons kan seën.

As daar sonde in 'n faset van my lewe is en ek wil dit nie laat staan nie, kan ek nie met enige greintjie geloof in my vir God vra om my in 'n ander faset van my lewe te help nie. God se spesiale liefde vir ons as sy seuns en dogters sluit in dat Hy ons dissiplineer wanneer ons in die gewoonte van ongehoorsaamheid verval. Want dit lei net tot 'n verlies aan vrede, om nie eens te praat van die verlies aan krag vir die volgende stryd nie.

Lank gelede, in die 4de eeu, het 'n leermeester en bekende liedskrywer, Efrem die Siriër, met groot wysheid opgemerk: "Dié wat nie die Here alleen wil dien nie, sal die slaaf van baie meesters word."[3] Om God se bepalings te verwerp stel ons nie vry om ons onafhanklikheid te geniet nie. Dit dompel ons eerder dieper in erge slawerny.

God roep ons liefdevol tot gehoorsaamheid. Hy gee nooit moed op nie. Sy heiligheid kan nie in gevaar gestel word nie. Wanneer ons aan Hom ongehoorsaam is, maak ons onsself seer en verbreek ons ons kommunikasie met Hom. Eers wanneer dit herstel is, kan ons sy seën op ons pogings ervaar.

3. Die bloedoffer moet altyd sentraal bly

Daar het nog iets by Gilgal gebeur. "Terwyl die Israeliete nog in Gilgal in die kamp was, het hulle die paasfees daar in die Jerigovlakte gevier, op die veertiende van die maand, in die aand. Die oggend na paasfees, presies op dié dag, het hulle ongesuurde brood en gebraaide koring, van die opbrengs van die land, geëet" (Jos 5:10-11).

Met die paasfees het hulle God se voorsiening en beskerming gevier. Die Hebreërs het 'n lam se bloed teen hulle kosyne gesmeer om die laaste plaag in Egipte te herdenk, toe die eersgebore seuns van hulle onderdrukkers gesterf, maar hulle eie kinders bly leef het. God het verklaar: "Waar Ek die bloed sien, sal Ek die huis oorslaan, en die vernietigende slag waarmee Ek Egipte gaan tref, sal julle nie tref nie" (Eks 12:13).

Slegs die bloed van Jesus Christus, wat 2 000 jaar gelede aan die kruis gestort is, beskerm ons teen God se fel oordeel oor sonde. Ons word nie regverdig verklaar op grond van ons goeie voornemens nie. Ons word nie beskerm weens ons trane en uitroepe om hulp nie. Ons kan inderdaad niks doen om God se guns te verdien nie. Net die bloed van Jesus bring ons in die regte verhouding met Hom. In die woorde van die lied van Andraé Crouch wat ons dikwels in ons kerk sing: Die bloed van Jesus reik tot aan die hoogste berge en vloei af na die diepste vallei. Dit is waarom dit nooit enige krag sal verloor nie.[4]

By die Brooklyn Tabernacle maak ons dikwels tyd sodat mense hulle verhale kan vertel en weer kan vertel, om te praat oor hoe God sy hand na hulle toe uitgesteek en hulle gered het toe hulle angsbevange was. Ons raak nooit moeg vir hierdie getuienisse nie. Ons aanvaar dit nooit as vanselfsprekend nie. Hierdie verhale lei inderdaad tot groot vreugde in ons gemeente. Ons verheug ons in dieselfde dinge wat God verheug. Sommige van hierdie verhale is dié van ons gemeentelede, en soms luister ons na die verhale van spesiale gaste wat ons na ons toe nooi. Ek wil hê ons gemeentelede moet altyd onthou die bloed van Jesus, God se Seun, reinig ons van elke sonde (1 Joh 1:7).

Ons het al meer as een keer vir Fernando Aranda van Kalifornië by ons verwelkom sodat hy van sy wonderbaarlike reis weg van hooploosheid tot by Jesus kan vertel. Hy het grootgeword in die ruwe buurte in die ooste van Los Angeles en was die jongste van vyf kinders. Van sy vroegste jare af was die aantrekkingskrag van die lewe op straat en die verleiding van dwelmmiddels sterker as enige invloed van sy ouers. Toe hy nog maar in die grondslagfase was, het hy gom begin snuif en deel geword van 'n bende wat baie ouer as hy was. Hy was maar agt jaar oud, toe was hy reeds bedrewe daarin om stokkies te draai, wat daartoe gelei het dat hy drie jaar lank in 'n verbeteringskool vir seuns geplaas is.

Toe hy elf jaar oud was, het hy teruggekeer na die gewelddadige buurt en by 'n gevaarlike bende aangesluit. Hy en 'n vriend is kort daarna in hegtenis geneem omdat hulle 'n man met 'n koevoet oor die kop geslaan het. Dit het "Fernie", soos hy bekend gestaan het, in 'n ander plek van aanhouding, vir jeugmisdadigers laat beland. Twee jaar later het hy as 'n volkome onbeheerbare jong seun na die strate teruggekeer.

Namate sy sestiende verjaardag nadergekom het, het Fernie twee interessante besluite geneem: om 'n ernstige verhouding met 'n meisie aan te knoop (nogal 'n leraar se dogter), en om by die Marines (die VSA se seesoldate) aan te sluit. Sowel sy oupa as sy pa het diens gedoen in hierdie afdeling van die weermag. In Fernie se geval het dit nie een van hierdie twee besluite goed uitgewerk nie. "My probleem as soldaat," sê hy vandag met 'n breë glimlag, "was dat daar op daardie oomblik geen oorlog gewoed het nie. Ek het toe maar sommer baklei met enigiemand wat by my was. Ek is vyf keer aangekla omdat ek geweier het om my aan gesag te onderwerp." Kort daarna is hy uit die vloot geskors.

> Ons word nie regverdig verklaar op grond van ons goeie voornemens nie. Ons word nie beskerm weens ons trane en uitroepe om hulp nie. Ons kan inderdaad niks doen om God se guns te verdien nie.

Intussen het hy sy jong vrou so kwaad gemaak deur sy wilde lewe dat sy hom eendag met 'n 25 mm-pistool in die hand geskiet het. Toe het sy hulle babadogter geneem en hom verlaat.

Maar Fernie was nie van plan om sy lewe reg te ruk nie. Hy het 'n ouer man ontmoet, wat "Folsom Eddie" genoem is weens sy lang verblyf in daardie spesifieke tronk in Kalifornië. Hy het vir Fernie 'n geleentheid aangebied om vinnig geld te maak. Hulle sou banke beroof en mense ontvoer. Al wat Fernie moes doen, was om die motor te bestuur waarin hulle vinnig moes wegkom.

Fernie se tweede vrou, Donna, het glad nie omgegee dat hy by hierdie soort bedrywighede betrokke was nie. Sy self is net so deur dwelms en vuurwapens bekoor soos haar man, en sy het inderdaad meer tatoeëermerke as hy gehad. Sy het egter woedend geword toe sy haar man een aand na 'n partytjie gevolg en hom betrap het waar hy met 'n ander meisie dans. Sy het hom met 'n mes in die rug gesteek.

Folsom Eddie en Fernie het hulle grootste slag geslaan toe hulle die president van 'n bank ontvoer, 'n kwartmiljoen dollar gekry en dit tussen hulle verdeel het. Eddie het egter 'n groot deel van sy buit in die kroeë van Los Angeles uitgegee, waar hy ook met sy kordaatstukke gespog het. Die polisie het gou op sy spoor gekom en albei mans begin soek.

Vroeg een oggend het Fernie en Donna by hulle baba gaan kuier, wat in Fernie se ma se sorg gelaat is. Nie een van hulle het verwag dat die polisie daar vir hom sou wag nie. Hulle het afluisterapparate in sy ma se telefoon geïnstalleer. Kort voor lank is dié jong man met 'n vonnis van 25 jaar tot lewenslank in 'n tronk in Noord-Kalifornië opgesluit.

Fernie se opstandigheid het egter selfs agter tralies voortgeduur. Toe drie gevangenes op die tronkterrein vermoor is, was Fernie een van die paar verdagtes wat in eensame aanhouding geplaas is. Elke dag het hy 23 uur lank niks behalwe die binnekant van sy sel gesien nie. Tydens die maandelikse ondervraging oor die moorde het hy net gemompel: "Ek weet g'n niks nie."

Op 'n dag het sy tenger en brose ma van 71 daar vir hom kom kuier. Toe sy haar seun sien wat met sy hande en voete in boeie aangeskuifel kom na die telefoon aan die ander kant van die koeëlvaste ruit, het sy in trane uitgebars. "Ek wil nie sterf terwyl ek jou in hierdie toestand moet sien nie," het sy huilend gesê. Maar gou was die besoekuur verby.

Fernie het ontsteld en radeloos na sy sel teruggekeer. "O God," het hy uitgeroep, en dit was waarskynlik die eerste gebed in sy lewe, "as U my uit hierdie put van hel sal haal, belowe ek om U my lewe lank te dien." Hy het glad nie begryp wat hy so pas gesê het nie. Hy het net geweet hy was op 'n spoor na nêrens en niks.

'n Jaar later is Fernando Aranda se naam sonder enige vooraf waarskuwing om twee-uur in die oggend uitgelees. Hy sou vrygelaat word. Dit moet 'n fout wees, het hy vir homself gesê. Hy het slegs dertien jaar van sy vonnis uitgedien. Dalk sou hulle hom tot in die woestyn neem en hom net daar skiet. Maar toe hy 'n paar uur later in die Greyhoundbus by die busterminaal klim, met skoon klere en 'n bietjie geld in sy sak, het hy besef dat hy regtig vry was.

Daardie aand het hy in El Monte, Kalifornië, van die bus af geklim. Hy was terug in sy ou woonbuurt. "Dit is verstommend hoe die Satan dinge vir jou kan reël," onthou hy. Nét daar by die terminaal was 'n man met die naam Robert. Fernie het hom meer as 'n dekade laas gesien. Robert het hom onmiddellik na 'n nabygeleë motel geneem, waar elke bekoring denkbaar, van dwelms tot meisies, gewag het. 'n Drie dae lange dronknes het hierop gevolg.

Die Saterdagoggend daarna was Robert en Fernie op pad strand toe om 'n kontakpersoon daar te ontmoet sodat hulle nog dwelms in die hande kon kry. Skielik het Robert gesis: "Pas op! Daar is die polisie se dwelmspan!" Fernie het sy geld en tronk-identiteitsdokument vir Robert gegee en na 'n nabygeleë park gehardloop. In die park het 'n klomp mense bymekaargekom om musiek te maak. Hy het gou in die groep verdwyn.

'n Man het na hom toe gekom en vir hom gesê: "Raai wat? Jesus is lief vir jou." Fernie het aanstoot geneem.

Maar toe het 'n man na hom toe gekom en, sonder om homself bekend te stel, vir hom gesê: "Raai wat? Jesus is lief vir jou."

Fernie het aanstoot geneem. Hy het onmiddellik omgedraai om weg te stap. Maar toe hy dit doen, het hy gesien hoe die polisie na hom toe aankom. Hy het besluit sy beste uitweg sou wees om weer deel van die skare te word – wat in werklikheid 'n openbare byeenkoms was wat geborg is deur Victory Outreach Ministries.

Wat volgende gebeur het, sou niemand ooit kon raai nie. Fernie vertel self:

> "Ek het nog nooit enigeen van hierdie mense in my lewe gesien nie. Maar 'n jong man met die naam Louie het na my toe gekom. Hy het amper soos die man in die Marlboro-advertensie gelyk – groot spiere, groot snor. Hy het tot by my gestap en dapper gesê: 'Haai, broer, kan jy dan nie die dag onthou toe jy in jou tronksel gebid het dat as God jou uit daardie put van hel sou vrylaat jy Hom jou lewe lank sou dien nie?'

"Ek kon dit nie glo nie! Ek was sprakeloos. Hoe kon hierdie man enigsins weet van die gebed wat ek langer as 'n jaar gelede gebid het?

"Dit het skielik vir my gevoel asof ek nie meer die stem van 'n mens hoor nie. Dit was die stem van God."

Maar voordat Fernie kon antwoord, het die man sy vinger direk na hom gewys en gesê: "En jy weet wat jy moet doen."

Dit was genoeg om Fernando Aranda net daar op die gras op sy knieë te laat neersink. Hy het begin huil. "Here, ek is jammer! Vergewe my al my sondes." Die krag van God het hierdie geharde misdadiger gedryf tot op die punt van volkome oorgawe.

Die volgende ding wat Fernie onthou, is die sagte vrouestem wat gesê het: "Kom ons neem hom huis toe." Hy het opgekyk en die meisie met die naam Georgina daar sien staan. Sy was die dogter van pastoor Sonny Arguinzoni, die hoof van Victory Outreach Ministries.

"Ja! Neem my huis toe. Asseblief!" het hy gekerm.

Binne oomblikke het die bedieningspan hom in 'n motor gelaai en in die rigting van sy ma se huis begin ry. Maar toe hulle ongeveer twee kilometer ver gery het, het hulle by Victory se tuiste vir mans stilgehou, waar meer as 50 mans in daardie stadium na 'n nuwe lewe saam met Jesus gelei is.

Fernie se ma het uiteindelik daar vir hom gaan kuier. Die beeld van haar seun in boeie was toe tog nie haar laaste beeld van hom nie. Sy het gesien hoe haar seun totaal hervorm is deur die reinigende bloed van Christus. Ná drie jaar se intense opleiding het Fernie by evangelisasieveldtogte, kerke en ander uitreikaksies begin optree om sy verstommende verhaal te vertel.

Wanneer hy vandag sy lewensverhaal vertel, sluit hy dit soms af met die meesleurende gospellied wat Johnny Cash bekendgemaak het: "My God is Real". Gehore – ook dié by Brooklyn Tabernacle – huil wanneer hy hierdie boodskap uitbasuin:

"… He's real in my soul!
My God is real, for he was washed and made me whole!
His love for me is like pure gold,
My God is real, and I can feel him in my soul![5]

Die bloed van die Lam van God is sterk genoeg om die kettings van dwelms en misdaad te breek. Dit vernietig swak gewoontes, benarde sosio-ekonomiese omstandighede en slegte vriendskappe. Dit is die paasfees wat elke paasmaaltyd vervang en ons vrymaak van die straf wat ons verdien. Dit is die middelpunt van ons hoop en geloof in Christus. Dit is God se voorsiening vir al die dilemmas waarin ons ons bevind.

Wanneer ons ons anker in die drie lesse van Gilgal – dankbaarheid en lof vir al God se seëninge in die verlede, 'n opregte hart wat berou het oor sonde, en 'n vaste geloof in die verlossingswerk van Christus aan die kruis – staan ons presies op die plek waar God ons kan seën. Ons is gereed om die "beter toekoms" in te gaan.

HOOFSTUK 4

DIE VERGETENE

Op 'n koue en winderige Saterdag in Januarie 1969 het ongeveer 200 mense saamgekom vir 'n troue wat om sesuur in 'n beskeie kerkie in die Bay Ridge-omgewing van Brooklyn sou plaasvind. In die weste het die winterson reeds agter die torings en kabels van die nuwe Verrazano-Narrows-brug weggesink, wat die lug nog koeler gemaak het. Binne-in die kerk het die ligte egter warm gegloei en daar was pragtige rangskikkings van wit varklelies vir hierdie feestelike geleentheid.

Die 26-jarige bruidegom, wat as 'n personeelverteenwoordiger in die middestad van Manhattan gewerk het, het senuweeagtig voor in die kerk op sy pragtige bruid gewag. Sy, 'n ontvangsdame by 'n groot farmaseutiese maatskappy in die stad, het asemrowend gelyk in haar wit Spaanse trourok, met 'n lang sleep wat vanaf die tiara op haar kop, teen haar rug af en agter haar aan oor die grond gevloei het. Dié jong man en meisie was waarlik lief vir die Here. Hulle het gebid en die Here gevra om by hulle spesiale geleentheid teenwoordig te wees. Hulle wou hierdie dag onthou, nie net omdat die seremonie en vreugdevolle onthaal vlot verloop het nie, maar veral omdat God se seën op elke oomblik gerus het.

Die seremonie het 40 minute geduur en 'n hoogtepunt bereik toe die middeljarige leraar uiteindelik aangekondig het: "En nou mag jy jou bruid soen." Daarna het almal saam die slotgesang gesing, die bruidspaar is met confetti bestrooi, die foto's is geneem en toe het hulle na die onthaal vertrek. Die bruid se ouers het gereël dat die spyseniers 'n heerlike aandete in die kerk se gemeenskapsaal voorsit, en die gaste het by die pragtig versierde tafels aangesit.

Toe die pa van die bruid, self 'n leraar en 'n talentvolle sanger, opstaan om die mense toe te spreek, het hy nie 'n heildronk ingestel of grappies gemaak nie. Hy het net 'n paar opmerkings gemaak en toe 'n gewilde gospelliedjie van daardie tyd saam met klavierbegeleiding gesing. Dit was soos 'n gebed wat die pas getroudes hulle eie kon maak. Die woorde van die lied klink só (vry vertaal):

"Vul my beker, Here, ek lig dit op, Here!
Kom en les die dors in my siel;
Brood van die hemel, voed my tot ek niks meer nodig het nie –
Vul my beker, maak dit vol, en maak my heel."[1]

'n Atmosfeer van aanbidding het geheers onder die gaste wat daar teenwoordig was. Sommige het hulle oë uit eerbied gesluit, ander het hulle koppe instemmend geknik, party het hulle koffiekoppies eers neergesit en hulle hande in aanbidding opgehef. Gefluisterde gebede en lofprysings het deur die saal opgeklink toe hy die lied afsluit. Die byeenkoms was nie meer 'n vrolike partytjie nie, maar 'n lofprysingsbyeenkoms. Mense het tot God gebid om die pasgetroudes te seën en hulle lewe saam met die rykdom van sy Gees te vul.

Niemand wou graag die atmosfeer versteur wat so spontaan ontstaan het nie. Die bruid en bruidegom het stil daar gesit, hulle koppe in gebed gebuig. En toe het 'n vrou van iets in die dertig onverwags vorentoe gestap en voor hulle gaan staan. Sy het begin praat.

Eers het sy die Here se seën op die jong man en sy bruid afgebid, maar toe het haar woorde in 'n profetiese uitspraak verander, soos dié wat gereeld in Bybelse tye uitgespreek is. Sy het sonder 'n vooraf uitgewerkte toespraak gepraat. Dit het gelyk asof sy op daardie oomblik die inspirasie ontvang het, en sy het gesê: "Die hand van die Here rus op julle albei. God het julle vir sy spesiale opdrag gekies. Hy sal julle gebruik op maniere waarvan julle nie eens kan droom nie. Die dag sal kom dat julle voor derduisende mense sal staan en die boodskap van God sal verkondig. Julle invloed sal veel verder strek as wat julle vandag kan begryp. Julle sal die wêreld deurkruis en vir mense van die liefde en genade van Jesus Christus vertel."

Die vrou se woorde het gesaghebbend geklink, en tog het sy dit met 'n teer hart uitgespreek. Sy het afgesluit met die stelling dat God se guns op die pasgetroudes sou rus omdat hulle hulle in geloof aan sy leiding onderwerp. Toe sy stilbly, het 'n hernude golf van lofprysing aan God onder die gaste losgebars, en die bruid en sy bruidegom was albei in trane.

> Die vrou se woorde het gesaghebbend geklink, en tog het sy dit met 'n teer hart uitgespreek.

'n Paar minute het verloop voordat almal bedaar het.

Toe hulle die volgende middag op die vliegtuig op pad na Hawaii was, het die jong man diep nagedink: Wat beteken die vrou se woorde? Dit maak nie sin nie. Ons het albei werk in die sakewêreld; ons is geensins vir die bediening opgelei nie. Ons het nie eens daaroor gepraat om so 'n lewe te oorweeg nie. Hoe is dit moontlik dat al daardie dinge ooit kan gebeur? Toe hy 'n paar dae later met sy jong vrou daaroor praat, kon nie een van hulle die raaisel oplos nie.

Wie is nie daar nie?

Ek besef terdeë dat sommige mense so 'n gebeurtenis as godsdienstige dwepery kan afmaak, of as 'n emosionele nabootsing van verskynsels wat saam met die apostoliese era tot 'n einde gekom het. Maar ek kan bevestig dat hierdie verhaal waar is, want op daardie dag was ek die bruidegom en Carol was die bruid. Ek kan julle ook vertel dat elke woord wat die vrou op daardie dag gesê het, letterlik waar geword het. Ons het nie doelbewus probeer om haar profesie in vervulling te laat gaan nie. Eintlik het ons aanvanklik teen so 'n wending in ons onderskeie loopbane gestry. Wanneer ek egter terugkyk op wat God in ons jare in die bediening laat gebeur het, kan ek net tot die gevolgtrekking kom dat sy Gees iets belangriks op daardie huweliksdag wou sê, en Hy het 'n onopvallende maar gewillige vrou as sy boodskapper gekies. Sy was niks minder – en niks meer – as Ananias van Damaskus nie, vir wie die Here gestuur het om die blinde Saulus te gaan soek en vir hom van wonderlike dinge in sy toekoms te vertel (Hand 9). Sy was iemand soos die evangelis Filippus se vier ongetroude dogters wat "die gawe besit het om te profeteer" (21:9).

Wat nog belangriker is, is dat ek oortuig is daar sal baie meer sulke oomblikke in ons lewe plaasvind as ons meer aandag sou gee aan die Persoon wat ek soms "die Vergetene" noem. Christene het beslis respek vir die Persoon van die Heilige Gees, maar die meeste van ons dink nie dikwels aan Hom nie. Ons beplan ons toekoms en streef daarna om ons doelwitte te bereik in die hoop dat God alles wat ons aanpak, sal seën. Maar bitter min mense is bewus van die lewende, werkende Gees van God wat wag om sy regmatige plek in ons lewe in te neem.

Hierdie ingesteldheid was 'n probleem onder God se volk deur hulle hele geskiedenis heen. 'n Soortgelyke probleem het Josua byna laat struikel het. Die Bybel vertel: "Josua was naby Jerigo. Toe hy sien, staan daar 'n man voor hom met 'n ontblote swaard in die hand. Josua het na hom toe gegaan en hom gevra: 'Is u aan ons kant of aan ons vyande s'n?'" (Jos 5:13). Josua het aangeneem hy is die

> Josua het aangeneem hy is die senior bevelvoerder. Maar wie was hierdie man wat so onaangekondig daar opgedaag het met 'n swaard in die hand?

senior bevelvoerder. Moses het al gesterf; Josua was in bevel. Hy het reeds Jerigo, wat op die horison sigbaar was, as die eerste en vernaamste teiken geïdentifiseer. Hy was gereed om met sy eerste belangrike aanval op die Beloofde Land te begin. Hy was waarskynlik senuweeagtig en het beslis gebid terwyl hy gewag het vir die geveg om te begin.

Maar wie was hierdie man wat so onaangekondig daar opgedaag het met 'n swaard in die hand? Wat het hy daar gemaak? Aan wie se leër het hy behoort?

"Vriend of vyand?" het Josua geblaf.

Is dit nie ongelooflik dat Josua amper lus gelyk het om te vég teen die Besoeker wat in werklikheid sy sleutel tot oorwinning was nie? Ons doen vandag so dikwels dieselfde dwase ding. God verskyn midde-in ons situasie en ons bevraagteken senuweeagtig sy identiteit, eerder as om sy magtige teenwoordigheid raak te sien.

Die res van hierdie verhaal in die Bybel is goed bekend. Die Vergetene het dadelik Josua se vraag beantwoord:

> "'Nee,' sê die man, 'ek is die aanvoerder van die leër van die Here. Daarom is ek hier.' Josua het diep gebuig en vir die man gesê: 'Wat wil u aan my, u dienaar, sê?' Toe sê die leëraanvoerder van die Here vir Josua: 'Trek jou skoene uit, want die plek waarop jy staan, is 'n gewyde plek.' Josua het dit gedoen" (5:14-15).

Die Bybel gee nie vir ons enige bykomende inligting oor hierdie "aanvoerder van die leër van die Here" nie – ons weet nie of dit Jesus voor sy menswording was, en of die Here God Hom op 'n spesiale manier geopenbaar het nie. Ons weet nie, en dit is waarskynlik nie nodig dat ons weet nie. Dit is baie belangriker dat ons sal besef hierdie hemelse Persoon is *ernstig onderskat* en *byna misgekyk*. Aanvanklik het Josua nie die vaagste benul gehad wie daar voor hom gestaan het nie. Hy het glad nie gedink dié persoon is belangrik nie. Hy het nie besef hoe dringend nodig hy die Besoeker se hulp gehad het nie. Maar hy het gou uitgevind.

Nie net 'n "Gees" nie

Christene vandag betoon eerbied aan God die Vader, en ons bring welverdiende lof aan sy Seun, ons Verlosser. Die Persoon van die Drie-eenheid wat egter gereeld in ons liedere, ons gebede en ons preke afgeskeep word, is die Heilige Gees. Hy is nie die een of ander vormlose vloeistof of gas nie; Hy is 'n Persoon en bestaan vir ewig saam met die Vader en die Seun. Hy was van die begin af by God en die Seun. Genesis 1:2 sê baie duidelik die Gees van God het in die begin van die skepping oor die waters gesweef.

Dié wat graag die King James Version van die Bybel lees, lees dikwels van die "Holy Ghost". En dalk is dit deel van ons probleem. As kind het ek dié uitdrukking 'n bietjie vreesaanjaend gevind. Ek het geen begeerte gehad om 'n spook te leer ken nie, of Hy nou heilig was of nie.

Maar Engelse Bybelvertalings het lank gelede reeds hierdie hindernis weggeneem deur die Naam "Holy Spirit" te gebruik – "Heilige Gees". Hy is nie die een of ander vreesaanjaende verskynsel nie. Hy is 'n Persoon, en alle gelowiges moet die begeerte hê om Hom te leer ken en Hom te volg. Hy is 'n lewende wese wat gevoelens ervaar en met God se mense praat. Ons lees dit herhaaldelik in die Nuwe Testament. Ons glo dat Jesus, toe Hy na die hemel opgevaar het, die Heilige Gees in sy plek gestuur het om by die dissipels te wees. Net soos ons Here belowe het, het die Gees met sy lewenskragtige bediening in die vroeë kerk begin. Die Nuwe Testament stel dit só:

> "Toe hulle op 'n keer bymekaar was om die Here te dien en om te vas, *het die Heilige Gees gesê:* 'Sonder Barnabas en Saulus vir My af om die werk te doen waarvoor Ek hulle geroep het" (Hand 13:2.)

"Die Gees sê uitdruklik dat in die eindtyd sommige afvallig sal word van die geloof. Hulle sal misleidende geeste navolg en die leerstellings van bose geeste aanhang" (1 Tim 4:1.)

"Luister daarom na *wat die Heilige Gees sê:* 'Vandag, as julle sy stem hoor, moet julle nie hardkoppig wees nie, soos julle voorvaders toe hulle in opstand gekom het …'" (Heb 3:7-8.)

"Elkeen wat kan hoor, moet luister na *wat die Gees vir die gemeentes sê* (Op 2:7.)

Ons moet fyn oplet na die Gees se woorde, net soos die gemeente in Antiogië, van wie ons so pas gelees het. Die oomblik toe die Gees vir Barnabas en Saulus vir die bediening uitgesonder het, het die gemeente nie bloot aanbeweeg na die volgende item op die agenda van 'n vooraf vasgestelde erediensvolgorde nie. "Nadat die gemeente gevas en gebid en hulle die hande opgelê het, het die gemeente hulle laat gaan" (Hand 13:3).

Dit is een van die belangrikste take van die Heilige Gees: Hy werf mense vir die werk van die koninkryk. Hy laat dinge gebeur sodat die doelwitte van die Vader bereik kan word. Hy rus gewone mans en vroue toe om buitengewone dinge te vermag. As ons dit nie glo nie en ongevoelig raak vir die stem van die Heilige Gees, sal ons wonderlike dinge misloop wat God vir ons beplan het. Ons sal vasklou aan blote feite en teorieë oor die Here sonder om ooit die krag van God in ons lewe en omstandighede te ervaar.

Die Gees was ook aktief aan die werk in die tyd van die Ou Testament. Ons gaan nou na slegs vier van dié vele geleenthede in die boek Rigters kyk, oomblikke toe die Gees mense toegerus het om heldedade vir God te verrig.

Otniël

Die eerste persoon is Otniël, 'n neef van die beroemde Kaleb, wat een van die twaalf spioene was wat uitgestuur is om Kanaän te gaan verken voordat die Israeliete die land ingeneem het. "Die Gees van die Here was op hom en hy het oor Israel geregeer. Otniël het oorlog gemaak teen koning Kusan-Risatajim van Mesopotamië, en die Here het hom oorgegee in die mag van Otniël. Hy het vir Kusan-Risatajim verslaan. Daarna was daar veertig jaar lank vrede in die land, en toe is Otniël seun van Kenas dood" (Rig 3:10-11).

Hierdie militêre oorwinning was geen geringe prestasie nie. Die Israeliete is redelik lank deur hierdie naburige koning geboelie en rondgestamp. Otniël het opgestaan en die situasie omgekeer – 40 jaar lank. Stel jou enige politieke leier vandag voor wat sy of haar werk so goed doen dat die land die volgende 40 jaar lank geen ernstige konflik ervaar nie. Hy of sy sal 'n nasionale held wees. Skoolkinders sal later stories oor hom of haar skryf. Sy of haar gesig sal ongetwyfeld op die vernaamste munt of geldnoot verskyn. Dit is wat Otniël vermag het – omdat "die Gees van die Here" op hom was.

Gideon

Die tweede persoon in Rigters wat ons moet raaksien, is die skaam en bang Gideon met die swak selfbeeld. Hy het grootgeword met die oortuiging dat hy 'n nikswerd is. Dit lyk asof hy bestem was om die klassieke voorbeeld van die onderpresteerder te wees. Hy het niks van homself verwag nie, selfs nie eens van enigiemand anders in sy familie nie. Toe 'n Engel dus eendag daar opdaag en hom 'n dapper man noem wat die Midianitiese onderdrukkers sou verdryf, het hy met tientalle verskonings gereageer. Hy sou nooit enigiets betekenisvols kon doen nie, het hy vir die besoeker gesê.

Maar namate die tyd verloop het, het Gideon ontdek dat die teenoorgestelde waar is. En toe breek die oomblik uiteindelik aan: "Die Gees van die Here het vir Gideon in besit geneem, en hy het die ramshoring geblaas en die Abiësriete opgeroep om hom te volg. Hy het ook boodskappers na Manasse, Aser, Sebulon en Naftali toe gestuur en hulle ook opgeroep om hom te volg, en hulle het almal bymekaargekom" (6:34-35). Wie, Gideon? Hy het nog nooit beheer oor enigiets in sy lewe geneem nie. Maar nou het die Heilige Gees hom bemagtig, en binne twee dae het die Israeliete 'n verstommende oorwinning behaal.

Jefta

Die derde leier is die onbekende Jefta. Dit was natuurlik nie sy skuld dat hy gebore is as gevolg van sy pa se besoek aan 'n prostituut nie. Sy halfbroers het hom verag en hom goed laat verstaan dat hy nie by die res van die familie inpas nie. Uiteindelik het hulle hom verstoot en hy het "'n klomp leeglêers" om hom bymekaargemaak om sy bende te wees (11:3). Uit verskeie opmerkings wat hy gemaak het, kry ons duidelik die indruk van 'n man wat liggeraak was. Hy het gepraat voordat hy gedink het.

Maar toe die volk in die moeilikheid beland en dringend 'n leier nodig gehad het, het die leiers na Jefta toe gegaan. Op daardie oomblik "het die Gees van die Here op Jefta gekom, en hy het deur Gilead en Manasse getrek en verbygetrek tot by Mispa in Gilead, en van daar af het hy teen die Ammoniete opgetrek … en die Here het hulle in sy mag oorgegee" (11:29, 32). Die Gees se salwing was sterker as sy eienaardighede en menslike swakhede.

Simson

Laastens is daar natuurlik Simson – wat van sy geboorte af uitgesonder is om God te dien en boonop buitengewone liggaamlike krag ontvang het om dit te kon doen. Maar wat Simson namens die Israeliete vermag het, was meer as om bloot armspiere te laat bult. *Vier keer* sê die Bybel iets anders oor hom:

"Die Gees van die Here het hom … begin lei" (13:25).

and there were severe differences among provinces, with some at a shockingly low level.[41]

It is worth pointing out that the SACMEQ Grade 6 tests also showed that the top 20% of schools in South Africa are outperformed by their Kenyan counterparts. It could certainly be argued that the filtering and throughput rates in Kenya are more stringent, and thus select the better students at the higher grades. Nonetheless, the statistic does prevent any major outburst of arrogance about standards in our moderately better-performing (ex-white) schools.

Fleisch shows what this means for specific schools, beginning with the example of a Vryburg school in the North West.

> Of the 21 Grade Six learners who were assessed, four were reading at a pre-reading level, ten were reading at an emergent reading level, and seven children were reading at a basic level. At this particular school, none of the children who were assessed had begun 'reading for meaning'. The situation in mathematics was even more serious as half of the learners tested were at the pre-numeracy level, the others achieving only one level up at the emergent stage. In contrast, at a school attended by the most affluent children in the provincial capital of Limpopo, the Grade Six learners all demonstrated that they could read and do mathematics extremely well. Thirteen of 18 children tested were reading at the highest levels possible, and 11 were at the highest mathematics level, i.e. abstract problem-solving.[42]

South Africa has the lowest score in the Progress in Reading Literacy Study 2006 (PIRLS)[43], administered by a University of Pretoria team. This is despite the fact that South Africa tested Grade 5 learners against Grade 4 in other countries. (South African learners were a full year older than those in other countries, yet they failed to perform.) South Africa is way below the norm, with extremely poor results. The test is completed in the home language and 72% wrote in an African language.

The average achievement for South Africa was significantly lower than that of every other country assessed. The reading scores of South Africa, an upper-middle income nation, are severely below those of even lower-middle income nations. Although some children read at adequate levels, the average South African score was 302. The international average was 500.

The PIRLS study of 2006 only confirmed the findings of all the other tests – that South Africa comes at the bottom of the pile and that our children are just not hacking it when it comes to reading and maths at very basic levels. One report for a corporate funder showed stick figures in rows of ten being painstakingly crossed out in an attempt to bring order into a simple subtraction sum as mathematical formulae and processes were reduced to basic manual counting.[44]

So, how many South African students would be performing at the same standard as the top 75% in developed countries? Only 10% of SA students match the top 75% in literacy. This falls to 6% for both maths and science. This means that from a labour market point of view, South Africa lies far behind global counterparts.[45]

At a matric level, there are a few simple ways of pointing out the inequalities. Nick Taylor, head of the Joint Education Trust and a former mathematics teacher himself, uses maths passes to indicate performance and output. He shows that 79% of high schools fall into the poorly performing category, producing 15% of the total of higher-grade passes in mathematics, while two-thirds of the passes are produced by just 7% of the schools.[46]

The simple ratios below show how there are severe inequalities between black and white at matric level. For every black A-aggregate matriculant, there are eight white ones even though black matriculants in general outnumber white matriculants by twelve to one. Whereas 10% of white matriculants achieve an A-aggregate, just 0.1% of black matriculants do.[47]

It is true that there are criticisms of tests. Critics ask whether tests can really prove who is the brightest and the best. Sometimes a learner's ability to write tests is being tested. Tests have cultural implications; there are language barriers that may reflect how he or she answers questions set at an international level. All these questions are valid. Yet many of the children in other countries, often in similar poor households in middle-income countries, suffered many of the same disadvantages. Even in Malaysia and Singapore, both high-end performers, children were not always writing in the language of their homes.

Furthermore, these tests do represent a set of benchmarks and give some kind of cut-off to global achievement. If one wants to enter the mainstream, there is little way to challenge its outlines without first performing within its systematic parameters. In addition, all sorts of anecdotal evidence suggest that the tests are a reasonably true representation of how cutting-edge our skills levels are (or are not) and of the serious problems in the ability of our children to perform simple reading and mathematical functions, crucial for competing and interacting in a modern, globalised world.

Other important measures relate to progress through the system, how well the schools retain learners and what the dropout rates and throughput pass levels look like. While in 2007 whites achieved a 52% exemption rate, allowing passage to university, this rate was only 11% for black students – virtually the same as in 1991, admittedly for a much smaller group. Yet, in the same year of 2007, 39% of blacks failed as against less than 2% of whites.[48]

The Millennium Development Goals are a set of United Nations development goals, with agreed targets set by heads of government at a special UN Millennium summit. For education, they call for universal primary education and gender equality at primary school level. On both key counts we have close to met these goals. Yet it is quite clear that millions of children are not progressing through the school system. It is estimated that perhaps only 52 of every 100 who start Grade 1 make it to Grade 12.[49] Numbers of learners matriculating today are really not much greater than in 1994, with similarly poor higher-grade maths and university-exemption passes.

The Institute of Race Relations (SAIRR) suggests that only half of the roughly one million children who were in Grade 10 in 2006 wrote their new Outcomes-based Education matric exams in 2008. Of that group, only 30% actually passed to the end of matric, while only 8% passed the new mathematics exam.[50]

As Taylor says: 'Hundreds of thousands of our children leave our schools every year without the foundation skills needed to benefit from further education or to secure anything but the most menial jobs. More disturbing is that dysfunctional schools are unable to socialize young people into the attitudes of mind required for citizenship in a democracy . . . school leavers are easy prey to a life of crime, poverty, corruption and inefficiency.'[51]

Stats, guesstimates and beyond

You have to admit that this evidence is not conclusive. It is patchy. It is not detailed enough to work out exact correlations and causes. It does not tell us much about changes over time, and about exactly how and where the system may be improving or be in decline. But it does suggest that something is seriously wrong.

Some commentators do not like anyone being too dramatic about the facts and figures we have looked at in this chapter, suggesting that it does not help to be too critical about the conclusions that are drawn from the statistics. Others, like me, disagree. If you cannot name the problem, if you cannot face up to it and say how bad the situation is, how are you ever going to deal with it? Take a deep breath. Say that things just are not what they should be. We are not where we would like to be and need to find out the reasons, the problems, and the challenges that we can deal with. Then we can develop a plan.

It has taken a while for this message to filter through. Over the last few years, more and more observers have used the term 'crisis' to comment on and describe the school system. If it is this bad, if it is this bad relative to even middle-income countries in the rest of the world, if it is this bad for most children relative to a small group that does OK in South Africa, if it is this bad relative to what the country needs – is this not a state of crisis?

The term 'crisis' may not mean that everything is falling apart. It may not mean that ceilings are falling in and school gates are hanging on their hinges – though this is happening in many cases, as far as we can tell. It may not mean there is total chaos in the school day and nowhere even the semblance of a normal school routine exists. 'Crisis' means, simply, there is a situation that is far from desirable, that is creating severe problems, and that is hurtling us at speed towards a real abyss. It is a crisis of outcomes, of delivery, of expectations, of dashed hopes and closed opportunities.

Some have also objected to the majority of schools being called dysfunctional. I always use the following analogy. Imagine the family sits down to supper together. They are all there, mother, father, son and daughter, and food is served on the table. The family may even appear completely functional. Yet after dinner, the father never washes up, in fact he is soon involved in drinking and beating his wife. The girl goes off to her room and injects herself with drugs. The boy is out with his friends till late, stealing hubcaps and breaking into houses, laughing as he learns to use a knife to impress his peers. Is the family really functional? There are some pegs on which to hang your hopes, but the implications of denial are ultimately more serious.

Two recent comments by education experts raise some very interesting questions about what we truly know about education in South Africa. Take note, the following arguments are in two totally disparate areas of education, and separate specialisations for researchers. But they are both key areas of decision-making in public life and education implementation.

The first area is about the impact of how we spend our money in education, especially whether we are contributing to building equity, a widely accepted if much argued about goal of our society. The second area is about how we go about ensuring quality in our education system and how appropriately to measure whether the system is working, whether it is getting the quality outcomes desired even in relation to its own set goals. What would be appropriate ways of going about measuring outcomes (exams?) and what kind of institutions help a focus on quality (SAQA?)

Former head of the Wits Education Policy Unit, Shireen Motala, makes an important point about the limitations of the literature on school finance equity. This literature is about how to spread limited education finances so as to achieve goals of equality and fairness, in this case including a pro-poor bias to make up for past disparities.

> The literature is small in scope, and in general lacks methodological and conceptual rigour. Much of the valuable work is written in the form of policy briefs and observations are not based on in-depth, sustained research. Other work is limited in that it measures the impact of one variable – socio-economic status – and is less explicit about its methodological approach. The contribution of education economists has focused largely on the human capital approach and its linkages to economic growth. While useful, it does not directly contribute to questions about equity of inputs disaggregated to the school level. The absence of a strong tradition in the area of school financing continues to result in limited knowledge for education planning. While the contribution of rigorous theoretical and conceptual policy reviews must not be underestimated, they tell us little about events on the ground. [52]

This is a strong and potentially scary argument considering that education is the largest part of the national budget, and issues of where you put your money and how it is spent are of wide concern and have a big impact. Motala essentially says we know just about nothing.

A completely different area is that of quality assurance, one on which every citizen has a comment, for example, 'the standard of education has really gone down since . . .'. As indicated in the next few paragraphs, it is nonetheless an area in which it is not clear that much useful is being contributed.

Quality assurance is one arena where government has often been accused of setting up wasteful bureaucratic structures. Young up-and-coming researcher Stephanie Allais has looked closely at some of the standard-setting and accreditation arguments, and the bodies set up to ensure quality in exams such as matric (Umalusi), higher education (HEQC) and work-oriented skills (the SETAs). We probably all have opinions on at least one of these bodies, or at least the results in the arena where they operate.

She argues that the time and expense can be justified only if there is proof that various quality assurance systems will monitor and improve educational quality.

> However, there is often little evidence that this is the case. Some people argue that the time and money spent on quality assurance would be better spent directly targeting factors that affect quality in educational institutions – improving salaries of teachers and lecturers, improving libraries and facilities, and so on.
>
> Since quality assurance in education is relatively new, there is very little research into its effectiveness. Those in favour of quality assurance sometimes assume that it will improve quality because that is what it is designed to do. However, good intentions do not always lead to the desired objective and sometimes good intentions have undesired consequences. [53]

Allais seems to be arguing that a whole slew of decisions have been made in South African education without much evidence to suggest they should have been chosen or were the best decisions to achieve the desired results.

Right through the conclusions of all sorts of commentators and a range of researchers, there is a constant refrain: there is not actually enough evidence. How do we make our way through this?

The truth is that we have a range of statistics. It is also true that the data is not altogether consistent. We do not often have information collected over a number of years, to compare what happened over time. The existence of the homelands in the bad old days of apartheid cut off millions of South Africans – often the poorest and most disadvantaged – from being measured as a part of South Africa. So it is quite hard to argue seriously about trends. While some few correlations may be possible in small slices, we often cannot draw decisive and final conclusions, certainly not about the actual causes and effects of the areas that appear to correlate.

In addition, it has recently become difficult to examine racial bias and racial differences in performance. More than that, what used to be 'white schools' often have significant numbers of black learners, as evidenced by the taxis flowing from townships to better schools in the suburbs every school day.

Surprisingly little detailed work has been done on quantifying and understanding these shifts. There is often very lazy analysis, as when black kids in former model-C schools are neatly categorised as 'middle class'. Why? Because they attend schools that charge fees? Because the schools give a reasonably good education, or are located in middle-class suburbs? The schools may well not be taking the poorest of the poor, but surely it is the children of domestics in their employers' homes, or children from townships whence the middle classes proper have long fled, who are trying to benefit from some of the advantages of schools that traditionally served more middle-class and white children?

Like the rest of the transition in South Africa, such important shifts in demographics, in class dynamics, in access, have often been left to be the stuff of urban legend, shallow prejudices and political posturing or preconceptions.

Nor do we always know if things are simply happening at the same time due to a common outside cause, or if they are the direct reason for the behaviour and results of each other. Academic researchers operate on the basis of their individual interests and curiosity, there is a lack of general direction or priority in the social discourse, and there is an ad hoc nature in many universities' approaches. All of these have their causes and are often very positive things in themselves.

The result has often been interesting snippets, a lot of people doing a lot of bits of research, but little coherence. There is no tradition of widespread randomised trials, which are difficult to set up anyway, that also explore enough of the affected population to test whether assumptions actually do make sense and work to scale on the ground. What goes on in the classroom is also often anybody's guess, yet this is frequently one of the most important sites of learning.

Are we on our own? If there is no final and conclusive proof of anything, can we say whatever we like? Is it just luck that we get it right? Is policy-making purely coincidental, a case of who gets together, who has influence, and what their common assumptions turn out to be? A cynical view might not be far off these things, to be honest.

Nonetheless, we get by in life with less than perfect information. We collect the best we can. We put it together to see if we can make a coherent argument. We see if there is enough information to be credible in making these arguments. And then we put forward our case. If necessary, we argue for decisions and actions. Waiting for perfect research and information is like waiting for Godot.

But of course we have to say this with caveats. We cannot ignore facts and research that seem to go against the grain. We must have a coherent framework, which is up for scrutiny. It is always good to strive for more and better research. We must encourage the education departments, NGOs, professional researchers, project leaders, individuals and institutions like schools to make data available and for there to be systems and places where such information can be acquired and gathered.

For example, the Department of Education has set up the National Education Infrastructure Management System (NEIMS) to get information on what is going on in schools, including physical infrastructure – obviously with a host of data-gathering problems, such as untrue information, or the suppliers of information not getting feedback or seeing the use of this research.

This is not meant to be a treatise on the limitations and requirements of research: just a plea to breathe in and accept that things are not always adequately defined, counted and measured, nor properly processed and presented in the real world. The uncertainties of the modern world might be enough to make the most hardened believer in statistics, research and information wonder whether science is only relative. Perhaps spirituality or guesswork or horoscopes are also effective tools for making decisions.

But we need to be careful that this is not an excuse for mediocrity or an argument against doing the best we can in relation to research. We do not have to give up on knowledge and science. Rather, we should put on our 'crap-detectors', not get intimidated by flashy tables or graphs, and consider the need for a methodological warning that readers should be on their guard.

This is also an argument for us not to be arrogant, whether we are arguing based on our own experience, or whether we are drawing on much wider samples of the population and more systemic conclusions. In both cases, it helps to be humble and understand the limitations of the positions argued. In both cases, we will not be able to throw facts at someone to prove our point decisively. Like the rest of social arrangements, so in education too, compromises, improvements and assumptions will have to be suggested, built and tested if we are finally to get agreement on how to go forward.

We just have to get on with our lives. We can hardly sit around paralysed in absolute fear of making choices because we do not have absolute information or absolute certainty. Absolute certainty is in any case often a guesstimate even when information and data seem very sound.

There is probably enough information, anyway, to draw the firm conclusion that the outputs of the South African education system are not adequate or good enough. We could of course argue forever about who defines 'good enough'. Rather let the context of the argument set the implicit assumptions so that they can be discussed or challenged.

Causation is even more vexed. Whether inadequate results and outcomes are the result of bad government choices, or who is to blame, or what are the exact causes, is another matter. These questions will certainly be part of the discussion later when I take the position that it is a multitude of causes that help create the complexity and difficulty of education. It is how this multitude intersect to create a 'toxic mix' that is the real issue.

Still, despite uncertainty, I will put forward conclusions that lead to decisive recommendations for action and clear intervention areas. There is not going to be a cop-out on the basis of how little we truly know or how complex things are. We can so easily make the world more complex than it is; sometimes (not always) the simplest and the most common-sense arguments are the best.

Trapped in poverty

Apart from the serious inadequacies in the outcomes from our schooling system, there are other areas, both within and beyond the system, where the country appears to be failing its children. I will give further evidence of a host of challenges that impact on our schools and reinforce their poor performance in most cases.

For many of our children, the conditions of their daily lives mean they do not present themselves at the school gate in a position to learn. Communities and families have been devastated by the impact of apartheid and the legacy of poverty it has left. Even today, there are movements and shifts as communities travel from rural areas to peri-urban informal settlements or to escape the degradation of rural land and farming.

For a while – especially since 2001 when government's Growth, Employment and Redistribution strategy (GEAR) began to release more funds freed from debt to be used for social expenditure – poverty seemed to be lessening, especially among young people. Probably 50% of children lived in a situation of poverty; years of economic growth and widespread social grants, especially pensions and the child support grant, and the provision of electricity and water, were beginning to make some impact on this. But still, at least 25% of children sometimes or always go hungry, with this figure close to 40% in the Eastern Cape. Parents can barely buy food, let alone books or light.[54]

Now the world crisis has begun to bite. Factories and the services industry are closing down as demand slackens and exports dry up. Jobs are being shed on an increasing scale, despite the fact that South Africa has been relatively sheltered from the direct effects of the financial crisis. Now the world slowdown is having a drastic impact on the formal economy, on the money that individuals, communities and government have to spend. Children cannot escape the effects of this – it is likely to be a slide downhill for some years to come.

It is not just the parents who are unemployed. Youth unemployment is extraordinarily high in South Africa. First-time jobseekers without experience find it difficult to get work. Many communities report youth unemployment of 60% or higher. The evidence is that, without education, and often at least a matric, the stakes become even higher. In this kind of high-unemployment situation, however, there are many children who do have a matric or some lower-level qualification, but are unemployed nonetheless. Quite correctly, it becomes hard to convince children that education is a route to success. Why stay at school when it does not seem to help? The role models become the gangsters with flashy cars and gold chains, rather than children slogging away with their heads in books.

On the other side of these underworld opportunities are the reports in an HSRC survey of youth[55] that spoke of an overwhelming sadness among youth. They wanted to succeed and had all sorts of aspirations and hopes. Yet somehow they felt they would never make it through, that they did not stand a chance. They felt enormously sad as a result.

A film by a young American, Molly Blank, also captures some of this contradictory hope dashed and heartbreaking realism. Called *Testing Hope*, it follows the lives of four young people writing matric in Khayelitsha in Cape Town, their hopes, their families, and the sad reality of the schools to which they go and the quality of education they receive. They all live in conditions of poverty, yet they come over as children of great dignity and personality. We see them looking after younger family members or talking about how they would love to be able to buy their mother a house so she does not have to live in a shack forever.

They see education as the route out of their poverty and make tremendous sacrifices under difficult conditions to ensure a good matric result. In one scene, a young girl talks without bitterness about her school's lack of computers and her acceptance that other school-children nonetheless have computer laboratories that give them an advantage. We see the youngsters go to UCT to talk to an advisor about admission, and their shock discovery that their lack of a physics teacher – and therefore wrong subjects – will hobble their prospects of entry. As viewers, we realise how matter-of-fact the beautiful youngsters are about the inequalities of opportunity they face and the unlikely horizons of their lives.

Having no job means growing hunger. Lack of electricity and water makes it harder to study and takes priority away from 'luxuries' like educational support or expenditure. Parents anyway struggle to provide educational assistance, very often not having succeeded at school themselves. Of children with at least one parent who has attained less than Grade 10, only 30% gain a matric. This rises to 56% where one parent has Grade 10 or 11, 74% where a parent has matriculated, and 84% if a parent has a degree.[56] These are average levels of education the country has not yet attained, despite slow improvements in the average educational attainment levels.

Parents will lose jobs in the current crisis and be unable to feed their children. Purchases of items such as books and pencils, school uniforms, shoes to help with the long walk to school, simply become luxuries. Already, many children are nutritionally challenged and go to school without a square meal. The effects of malnutrition, lack of nutrients and physical stunting are long term. They directly affect children's ability to concentrate, and they create learning difficulties and disabilities.

There is too a psychological impact of dependence, of the loss of hope and possibility. Children are more and more likely to find no one in their homes who is working – they do not wake up to see a family member tying his or her shoes and setting off to the routine of a work day. As jobs disintegrate, so individuals and families are put under increasing stress. The order and regularity that establishes boundaries, discipline, that creates the structure and framework to improve their lives, is sucked away and slowly disintegrates further.

There are other ways in which children suffer from poor health. Parents are dying of AIDS so that many young children find themselves fending for family members, becoming heads of households at an early age. While AIDS is not necessarily as huge a factor among the very young as it is in the general population, at certain ages children will find themselves very vulnerable. Without hope, the AIDS message of protection is hard to sustain. Girls find themselves open to pressure from sugar daddies or older men with resources of some kind.

Then there are the basic diseases of poverty, especially widespread in the rural areas. Here health protocols are most often observed in the breach, especially given the deterioration in the health services over the recent past. In the Western Cape, there is extensive foetal alcohol syndrome in poor rural communities. Intestinal worms are common throughout South Africa, especially in the rural areas and former homelands.

Worms consume nutrition, they create tiredness and a lack of concentration. Emerging from the anus, they make it hard to sit and mean that kids are continuously itching. I remember a young researcher explaining the impact of worms to an audience of education academics from the English-speaking universities. He explained how as a Zulu speaker he had travelled the old Transkei areas, which are traditionally Xhosa-speaking, picking up faecal samples in small bottles for analysis at labs. Much of his time was taken up simply convincing the villagers that, though an outsider, he had no evil intent in collecting their samples of poo, and was involved in science not witchcraft.

His descriptions of the worms emerging had the academics wide-eyed. You could almost see them wriggling in their seats as he explained why it is so hard for kids with worms to concentrate. Consistent doses of deworming treatment could do much to increase the ability of children to concentrate and think about schoolwork at all.

There are many other similar diseases of poverty, not necessarily hard to treat, but which mean that children arrive at school with deep burdens to overcome even before they start thinking of learning and study.

In these kinds of conditions, with communities and families under dire stress, it is not surprising that things do not hold together. Sexual abuse and oversexualised responses from children are one symptom. Many schools report a lack of discipline and all sorts of psychological and traumatic responses in their children that make it difficult to establish authority.

There is a range of temptations and distractions. It is hard to say if drug taking has increased over the years, but certainly the availability of 'tik' (methamphetamines) and heroin has changed the situation and increased the dangers. There seems to be anecdotal evidence that in countries like South Africa, which become way-stations and transport routes in the drug trade, there is an increase in the amount of hard drugs that are flooding communities. There is also a greater chance of children being caught up as sellers and merchants, with a thriving drug culture providing attractive-looking opportunities.

Gangsterism has always been around. In the Western Cape, a gang culture has entrenched itself in communities, often linked to drugs, that provides far more of an attraction than schools ever could, and a range of social and peer pressures. Dysfunctional communities, often with high rates of alcoholism and drug use, have never recovered from the impact of the removals under the Group Areas Act that dumped families on the Cape Flats and removed their dignity through disenfranchising them in the 1950s.

Now, with drugs and social disintegration, gangs may well become more attractive as safe havens and institutions of protection, identity and belonging. Gangsterism and crime do provide certain disciplines and skills, make no mistake. Nonetheless, they are signs of negative and antisocial tendencies that seem to be on the increase. Direct and indirect involvement with gangs provides a set of social alternatives with largely destructive effects on learning, ranging from attendance and mental attitude to fear and actual physical injury, including rape. But it is hard to provide much concrete evidence of how seriously these things are affecting communities, or of their extent.

Every day, there are reports of attacks by fellow pupils on other pupils at schools, often using weapons such as knives. Teachers are threatened. Principals have been shot by gangsters or by jealous lovers, inside the classroom or at the school gate, as violence from outside the school intrudes onto the playground. The Human Rights Commission, in a set of hearings on school violence, uncovered that schools are often the place where pupils feel least safe. On the way to school, too, girls may be subject to harassment, physical attack and rape.[57]

Bullying and violence is clearly not something that just happens in black households or working-class schools. Recently, Parktown Boys, a well-known boys school in Johannesburg, suffered from media allegations of bullying and initiation practices. The reaction of parents was ambiguous, with one set of strategies to wear ribbons to school in solidarity with the boys who were the subject of discipline. The headmaster, faced with the divisions in the parent body, was himself equivocal and defensive.

In another incident, students from Reddam in Cape Town picked up an aspiring theatre youngster at a late-night garage and bashed his head against the side of another car, paralysing him for life. A mother in her four-by-four came to rescue the perpetrators and was only identified by the CCTV cameras. Again, at the end of 2008, police had to be called into a top private school in Cape Town because drunk youngsters celebrating the year end were terrorising the neighbourhood.

While neither of these incidents occurred on school grounds, they do – like the Reitz Hostel racial incidents in 2008 at the University of the Free State – raise wider questions as to whether the 'best' schools are necessarily ensuring the entrenchment of sound values and behaviours.

The resignations of a principal and senior officials at a leading Pretoria school on allegations of theft and corruption underline that the social breakdown and lack of borders and boundaries are deeply embedded throughout the society in which we live.

Such violence and ill discipline will make the task of teaching and learning that much more difficult, even for the most dedicated teacher or learner. There are often serious disruptions to the school day. Where life in the home or community is often anarchic or chaotic, with children the victims of disorder and violence, it seems that schools are not providing havens of stability and loving boundaries either. Without these, it is remarkable that our youth are so resilient and that so many of them nonetheless come through with unbroken hopes and aspirations for the future.

Hokkies and pit latrines

Schools are not even physically attractive places to be. The Department of Education has shown that some 41% of schools are in a poor or unacceptable state of maintenance. Backlogs, just basic catch-up, have been estimated at a minimum of some R153 billion.[58]

I have seen little *hokkies* for toilets, or plastic shelters falling down with broken doors where staff is expected to use buckets. Tiny bricks as seats stop little toddlers from falling into pit latrines in some rural schools. Facilities for washing hands may comprise a barrel that collects rainwater or is filled up, when it is remembered, by the municipal tankers. Basic hygiene, let alone dignity, becomes hard to maintain in these sorts of circumstances.

I have seen rooms set aside in some schools that are supposed to pass as staff rooms. In one corner is crammed a microwave to heat up food. Textbooks are stored against one wall, taking up most space. For teachers, there is a little corner of a table to leave their marking, to fill in their forms, and a tiny public space in which to counsel or motivate children they may have to speak to. Yet staff rooms are probably considered a luxury in the bigger scheme of things, certainly in the public eye.

The OECD commented on the number of schools made from mud, without lighting or facilities, and built by communities themselves, which collapse in the first rainfall or storms.[59] Many schools do not have sports fields. Schools are often physically unappealing, damp and cold, or overheated in summer, and with few facilities like computer labs or libraries that might possibly draw children willingly out of their homes.

Here are some examples of the backlogs in education infrastructure, based on departmental figures:

- 17% of schools have no access to electricity
- 19 940 (or 79%) schools have no library facilities
- 60% of secondary schools have no laboratory facilities
- 68% of schools have no computers
- 31% of schools depend for their water supply on boreholes or rainwater
- of the 9 461 schools with municipal water services, 6% depend on mobile tankers and 30% on communal standpipes
- 61% of schools with bucket or pit latrine systems have no sewerage disposal systems in place.[60]

So schools are not very inviting places, not places where pupils or teachers would want to spend their time. Pupils bring with them many of the evils and deficits of living in poor communities without vast resources, of broken homes and families, of poor nutrition and a terrible burden of hunger and disease. On top of all this, teachers themselves are often not prepared for teaching well.

No teacher, no school

There are nearly 400 000 teachers today, with some twelve million learners in about 27 000 schools. Not surprisingly, principals and the education districts are often unable to assume the burden of administrative and academic support required of them. Where would 27 000 managers come from, all capable of running schools well, with due regard for all the different levels of operation and skills required?

Schools are often not well organised, timetabling is poor, institutional process is arbitrary and ineffective. At a teaching level, haphazard planning and time management are often reflected in a poor ability to plan and timetable teaching plans for the curriculum over the year. Textbooks, a crucial resource, are not well used as part of a well-paced and phased teaching programme. In turn, this means that learners seldom have texts in their hands and even less to take home and work through.

We saw in Chapter 2 that teaching was often one of the very few jobs available to the black middle class, such as it was. There was massive expansion of numbers with the growth of extensive, lower-level Bantu Education schools, based on the quick-and-dirty training of the teacher colleges. It is hardly surprising that teachers today suffer from all the deficits that this second-class education was designed to achieve.

It includes poor levels of content knowledge, especially in maths and the sciences. Given the strictures, especially in these fields, there are not enough teachers. There are not enough maths teachers with advanced levels of agility and teaching methodology, there are in fact not enough maths teachers period, and they cannot be conjured out of the air. In all fields, there were not massive numbers of graduates through high school and beyond. Now the teachers are somehow expected to prepare the next generation of sophisticated, technologically savvy, cutting-edge knowledge workers. They do not have the skills.

None of this is to beat down on teachers. Teachers rightly feel there is a negative perception of their work; they do not receive public appreciation and support. Given the noble work that society has tasked them with, their morale is low. Many would leave the teaching profession if they could. The numbers responding to overseas job offers show the portability of many of their skills and their dissatisfaction in a sense with their conditions of work.

It has to be said that the core task of achieving adequate outcomes does not seem to be achieved. Yet there are undoubtedly thousands of teachers who work hard and diligently and love the children they try to serve. Teachers are a low-paid part of today's civil service, especially in relation to other government officials from assistant director and up. Their commitment appears low. They have felt confused by the demands of the new curricula embodied in Outcomes-based Education (OBE). The time spent directly on teaching is definitely lower in poorer schools than in better-organised schools in the suburbs. From increasing paperwork, to administration, to ill discipline, more time is taken up in non-teaching tasks.

Teacher training institutions, though well organised through the deans of education at the universities, have not put into the public discourse a clear set of debates about the direction and needs of teacher training, be it pre-service or while teaching (InSET). Just as among teachers, so among trainers there have no doubt been a number of quiet revolutions, but they have remained limited and contained. Issues such as labour relations disagreements seem to have taken up more energy and been prioritised in teacher union activities.

Of teachers, the OECD has said:

> Without greater and sustained attention to improving teacher education and aspects of the teaching career the prospects for success of the education reform agenda are limited. The teaching career does not enjoy a good public image, it is not attracting high quality candidates, initial and continuing education suffer from many deficiencies, the supervision of teachers' work is very weak, and the pedagogic supports are very inadequate in many schools. To bring about many of the reforms is an expensive and long-term task; but it is also an unavoidable one. [61]

More will be said in the next chapter about teachers. One of the key tasks of the new education dispensation will be finding the spark in teachers, helping to put in place joint and desired mechanisms for getting teachers able to teach as they know best, preparing them for a new world and the difficulties and needs of the students of today. Without doing this for and with teachers, all other attempts are doomed to failure.

Yet teachers are also not a blank slate who can be willed into superhuman achievements. Their problems and challenges should not be seen as accusations or blame, but as challenges that have to be faced and addressed in a planned and supportive but critical way.

Chapter 4 will look comprehensively at how the state has delivered and is delivering. It will look at the many achievements of government but also speak of the failings and blockages of the machinery of public support and delivery. At this point, I want only to refer to the well-known but little discussed fact that it is actually the provinces that are responsible for implementing national policies. It is the MECs (members of the provincial cabinet and thus politicians) and provincial education authorities who ultimately hold responsibility for what hits the ground.

The other point I want to make is that the direct support – curriculum, pedagogy, organisational and administrative – that you would expect to find either in a district office or among district officials appears to be thinly spread. Most education departments have consistently received qualified audits from the auditor general, signalling a range of administrative failures and ineffective controls or accountability systems. I will say more about these things when I examine the role of government later and its responsibility for the mess and disasters in which our schooling system finds itself.

I have only spoken about schools. Education of course is an integrated system, at best a pipeline of alternatives and choices. If, as I have argued, the basics do not seem to be in place, it is not surprising that a host of other areas of education go underserved. The kinds of problems I have already discussed find expression at various levels and institutions in the education system. Examples here would include the underresourced and little developed special needs education; the question of adult education or ABET (though a new campaign is under way, its full effects are to be watched with hope); and the much-vexed vocational training system. The latter includes workplace training and the Human Resource Development Strategy, mostly stuck between Education and Labour, with the really semifunctional, uneven and erratic SETA system and the National Skills Fund.

Overarching these, the quality control system under the SA Qualifications Authority (SAQA) reproduced bureaucratic inefficiency and seemed to hold back innovative development of teaching strategies, including a range of institutions that also might offer all sorts of second-chance opportunities to the millions of children who have fallen by the wayside of the schooling system.

Higher education has been underfunded and subject to the pressures of reorganisation and merger. While the demographics have shifted dramatically to ensure a new cadre of black admissions, the revolving-door syndrome has caused many black students to lack the academic and financial base to achieve academic success.

An HSRC policy brief tells us that the demographics of university attendance have shifted dramatically since apartheid. Compared with 37% white students in 1995, today the figure is 30%. Two-thirds of Wits' students, half of UCT's and a dismal 25% at Stellenbosch are black. [62] National Student Financial Aid Scheme (NSFAS) loans increased fivefold in the same period, signalling increased access and support for poor, rural and black students.[63]

Yet there are some disturbing counterfigures – half of all students drop out by their third year, and black African students fare the worst, with some institutions having dropout rates of up to 80%. At 15% of matric passes, our university admission rates are among the lowest in the world. Where we rank 32 on overall education spending, we rank 59 for spending on tertiary education.[64] The NSFAS pays only enough for a student to cover fees and perhaps a little more for books (in 2005 this was R10 000). We know that stories of students going hungry or unable to afford books or accommodation are real and ubiquitous, despite the urban legends of BMW-driving first-years who are always out on the prowl with a beer in hand.

We know, too, that access to university – despite the realities of even graduate unemployment – is a guarantee of economic privilege, of a good job and a good life. It is no wonder there is such desperation to ensure you are one of the 15% who gets a university place, that there are vicious and intense battles to prevent financial exclusions as the 50% dropout kicks in.

Despite the recent rises in university funding, reaching some R4.5 billion in special grants and subsidies, the HSRC argues that government appears to have decided the cost of getting working-class students to university is too high. 'Relatively low levels of public funding for tertiary education translate into higher fees, effectively shutting out the poor and reducing the ability of universities to contribute to social and economic development.'[65]

What this chapter has tried to focus on is the state of our educational landscape. It makes it clear that our schools are not achieving what they set out to do. The poor outcomes and low skills levels have implications and effects right through our economy and society. The spread from achievement to dysfunction means that vast numbers of our young people, indeed the majority, are shut out and do not receive the same opportunities as their richer, urban and often white brothers and sisters. Inequalities are reproduced in unsustainable ways. The effects are individual and are threatening our cohesion and sense of unity, our ongoing attempts to set dreams and to aspire to a better life.

The educational wasteland is deep and extensive. It touches the lives of pupils and their teachers, is affected by a range of factors at the school itself, by the quality of the teachers and the education departments' support for teaching and learning, and in the wider society.

At all levels, education does not seem to be performing. At best, it is not contributing much to the innovation this society needs to rise to the challenges it faces. At worst, it is contributing to dissonance and the many inequalities that continue to haunt our society and economy, that distort the possibility of realising the hopes and dreams of entire new generations of South Africans to come.

4 | The toxic mix: who is to blame?

A toxic mix of factors conspires to keep South Africa's schools in a state of disaster. Trying to find out where the fault lies is not a blame game. It is not about pointing fingers, but about looking the truth squarely up and down. It is about naming the problem and identifying the real causes, without fear or favour. It is about identifying levels of responsibility and influence, so that it is clear who can play a part where, and what difference it is likely to make.

No doubt some organisations and institutions will react defensively. Hopefully, others will see the issues as a set of challenges, as areas for debate, and possibly areas for action and intervention.

Some of the underlying reasons are historical and deeply sociological, a heritage that cannot be wished away but one that we will have to overcome and work with. Yet government clearly holds much responsibility for the mess. While there has been progress, there have been too many breakdowns and inefficiencies that will have to be tackled. Some of the factors are due to poor choices, sometimes made with the best of intentions, sometimes due to 'policy posturing' and politics rather than considered educational motivation. Poor implementation and inadequate accountability and monitoring systems have ensured that South Africa has a system that creaks and strains at various points.

The overoptimism of many education stakeholders on the one hand, and hand-wringing on the other, are also part of the problem. There are areas of responsibilities that are someone else's mandate and purview, it is true; there are historical causes that frame one's actions, it is true. Yet human beings and their institutions are not unchangeable or God-given. We are not victims. The past has an impact on us but it cannot weigh us down forever. Stakeholders, institutions and policy advisers will need to question their leadership and whether it has been up to the demands of the times. These matters, like others in the education terrain, will need to be subject to open interrogation and critique. Sacred cows such as the unions and their role in improving quality teaching will need to be analysed.

Undoubtedly, the past has influenced the present. The strands laid by Bantu Education – of bad mass schooling, poor teaching and conflicted classrooms – have pervaded much of the present terrain. Apartheid left a legacy of backlogs, structural poverty and inequalities. But there are key areas where human agency can make a difference. Thus, the role of teachers will be central.

What happens in and around schools?

It is clear, then, that together we must develop a common framework that will help us make sense of the disaster we see in education. This is essential because the nation will have to find a common thread of understanding to ensure common action. Differences in politics, approaches and key skills should be turned into strengths that are brought together – a difficult balancing act.

Chapter 3 gave us a feel of what is wrong, evidence of the many problems and challenges that seem to need fixing. But what is causing these problems? Are there central questions that come up over and over again, that seem to point to the real levers of dismal performance? Can we identify the most central factors that lead to poor performance and lack of quality? If we can, we are better suited to decide which interventions are most likely to work.

The first step to establish this common framework is to assert that these causal factors work together. It is not one by itself, but all of them together that conspire to hold back progress. This is the toxic mix, the poisonous brew that makes it so difficult to know where to start and what to do. I would argue that a set of actions must be seen as an integrated package, that coordination and a plan will be needed to ensure action at different levels at the same time.

This framework has been presented in one form in the multilayered model (already mentioned in Chapter 1), where UNESCO pointed to just how many factors influence education and have an impact on its outcomes. I argued then that we could usefully simplify the model to get more focus. The simplified framework suggested by Martin Carnoy, grandfather of education financing studies and professor at Stanford University, identifies three levels that are conceptually and practically separate, but all have high impact on schooling.[66]

The first level is the direct front line of interaction, the level where learning itself takes place. This is the level of the classroom, or what one could call 'in-school'. This is where the teacher faces the learner in an educational relationship, using his or her mastery of the subject and of the curriculum, her pedagogical and methodological training and instincts, to ensure that work is covered and the educational needs of the child are appropriately met.

The second level of concern is the structures around the classroom. These could be the systems, supports and organisation in the school, as symbolised by the management efficiency of the principal, but also the efforts of the districts and of the provincial and national departments. Do materials arrive on time, are schools maintained and repaired, are policies appropriate and do they help to support teachers so that they can be better in their primary task to ensure teaching and learning? This is the level of 'support to school'. It would include pre- and in-service training of the teacher, so that the teacher may appear in class in the best state to teach effectively.

The third level is societal. Are children adequately fed, do they have transport, what is their attitude to learning, how do gangs impact on schools? What is the feeling in society towards intellectuals and intellectual achievement? How do parents and stakeholders pull together to make sure that schools are properly funded and operate as they should? This third level defines the broadest level of interest by a society in what happens in schools. It also looks to effective coordination in the educational endeavour among a variety of government departments such as health, policing, social work, sports, culture and others.

As our tour of education faults in the previous chapter showed, there are likely to be serious problems at all three levels: the in-class level, the level of support to the school, and the societal level. The combination of problems and serious deficiencies in all three levels is noxious. This combination creates the toxic mix that has such devastating effects and is so hard and complex to turn around and change. And as we have already noted, this mix has been brewed in a poisonous atmosphere of a negative educational heritage from the past, and serious deficiencies and problems in the choices and processes of the present and recent post-democracy period.

Can we blame the struggle?

To what extent can we say the struggle is to blame for the current problems? Like many of the simplifications around education, there is a mixture of truth and ideological assumption in the question. In many cases, it is more about the attitude of the speaker to 'the struggle' than it is about understanding issues, causes, strands and legacies we may have inherited.

The assumption is often that the violence in education during the struggle years, the violent and disruptive responses of students in particular and the blows to order and stability, have created institutional instability that remains with us today as one of the features of our schools. Students became a law unto themselves, so that the culture of learning and teaching was fundamentally ruptured and the relations necessary for academic achievement were destroyed or severely damaged in this period. Hence the ANC and other liberation movements must answer for the tactics they employed in education.

The question is important. However, such kinds of counterfactual approaches are very difficult. Firstly, it is quite clear that Bantu Education did not achieve particularly magnificent outputs. It laid the basis for underfunded and underresourced mass education in the black communities, with poorly trained teachers as the educational leaders. So even if there had been no resistance or complaint, even no disruption, we have to ask what space we would find ourselves in today.

If students had simply kept their noses in their books, would Bantu Education today miraculously be producing the outputs it did not in any of the periods it existed? No one has suggested a natural upward improvement in the outcomes from the education system that apartheid put in place for black children. The ideological intentions of the time were clearly to create a passive and underskilled population, with the few skills being applied to 'own development' in the homelands.

The experience and outcomes of schooling in the homelands, even with varying degrees of independence or autonomy, are mixed, to say the least. Poor results were compounded by the broader issues of underserved rural education with all its problems. (Bophuthatswana under Lucas Mangope might briefly have provided an exception, but certainly any positive heritage has not been consolidated at all.)

Secondly, we could argue (though it needs much more work) that even the expansion that there was in Bantu Education – the rapid massification of education especially at a primary level – was itself partly a result of the resistance and complaints. Resistance to Bantu Education began on day one of its implementation in the 1950s, as we have seen. Thus expansion of schooling itself was often a response to dissatisfaction and an attempt strategically to outflank or undermine the complaints. Education resistance was always tied up with broader resistance and defiance of apartheid and its intentions.

Thirdly, we have to identify the bigger problem and ask where we locate the actual and significant disruptive effects that have had an impact on schools. For example, millions of homes and communities were disrupted by forced removals, poverty was deeply established in the structure of the modern economy, and issues such as suspicion of intellectual independence and often moderate middle-class elements were all deeply established in the psyche of resistance movements as a consequence of the need for deep solidarity.

If communities had just lain down and accepted apartheid and the education it offered, would communities have been any less disrupted and disintegrated than if they decided to rise up and challenge the system? Would teachers today find themselves any better qualified to teach if they had rolled over and accepted things? What numbers of teachers would have been produced without pressure from below to expand and even improve education? If children in the 1980s had accepted the police marching up and down the corridors to assert order, would academic results have been any better? Apartheid, especially apartheid systematically and successfully implemented, was bad for education. 'The struggle' was not to blame for this.

Apartheid ensured that education for blacks was bound to be conflicted, as well as second-class. Imposing Bantu Education as one of apartheid's key pillars, in a period in the 1950s when resistance and direct militant opposition were growing, was bound to be a recipe for disaster. Wishing it were otherwise, or secretly thinking that apartheid would simply have withered and disappeared organically with economic growth, is a strong political and ideological position. Once whites decided to fight it out, and resisted the possibility of negotiating acceptable transitions, the contours for disaster were set.

Another argument can be put forward. People who led school struggles might well have been the brightest and best of their generation, who simply could no longer accept the contradictions and injustices they saw. Many were children without structure and direction in their lives. In other circumstances (like today) they are the children who might well have found themselves in gangs or engaging in other antisocial activities.

Yet the struggle gave them a discipline, a sense of belonging, a respect for authority and a sense of moral and social boundaries that they were not going to get in other ways. At its best, such as when the NECC had mobilised parents and communities around the students' struggles, students were also led to better understand the crucial importance of education and building education alternatives. The tentative 'alternative' texts, the myriad study groups and the intensity of debate all suggest there was crucial learning and much leadership development in process.

The students of 1976 are no longer the disruptive children of today either; they are these children's parents and share many of the broad complaints about what schools are achieving. The disquiet and battles of the 1970s and 1980s do not simply translate into a continuity that can be identified as the root cause of problems today.

The many positive aspects of the struggle for students bear repeating, and are evident in a very different context for their militancy from today's apparent youthful war-talk. A positive view of COSAS's role in the Western Cape – and a practical picture of what student militancy in the 1980s meant – was quoted in Chapter 2. It suggested that the students' energy provided inspiration for awareness campaigns and coordinated initiatives such as cultural activities, interschool sports tournaments and winter schools, as well as more 'political' activities and support to worker struggles.

Yet these arguments do not mean that we cannot analyse the historical and institutional inheritance of the nature of struggle in the earlier period. Unsurprisingly, schools were often a 'battering ram' or at least the instigation point of many different kinds of resistance.

Let us accept that there was a social recipe in place that would only lead to disaster. If one were designing a recipe for an explosion, the government could not have done better. Here were institutions with obvious racial inequality, ideological in intent and housing large numbers of young people gathered in these sites daily. Together they could see the common and racially unequal situation in which they found themselves. Increasing progress through the system meant there were numbers of secondary students with the intellectual capacities to articulate their oppression. This combined with growing liberation successes in southern Africa as well as militant movements taking root, such as Black Consciousness and the workers' movement. The groundwork for the struggle for the schools, in the schools, was well prepared by the system itself.

Schools were bound to be a pressure cooker leading to agitation and action. Schools were unsurprisingly going to be part of the wider struggle. Today there is a lesson in this. The solution to education problems must at least partially lie in its integration with wider social objectives. The difference today, of course, is that the challenge is one of constructing a new society rather than tearing down and destroying the contours of the old.

Problems of discipline and authority today are constant refrains. The youth generation that emerged from 1976 was critical of adults and their alleged passivity in the face of apartheid. The actions of the youth based in the schools were a break with parents and an assertion of their autonomy and right to make decisions and take action.

We can speculate that this has given rise to a rupture that has never been repaired, that parents would struggle to reassert their authority over their children. At critical points parents certainly involved themselves in the affairs of the schoolchildren and in the wider community struggles – whether through the Black Parents' Association of 1976 under Winnie Mandela and Nthato Motlana, the NECC under Eric Molobi and Vusi Khanyile in the 1980s, or the shelter and training provided in camps in exile under the ANC or PAC.

Did these years of youth action, sometimes brutal and violent, give rise to the indiscipline and breakdown in lines of authority today? Are struggle techniques taught or handed down; do they just become a way of doing things that younger brothers and sisters pick up from their older siblings?

Initially in the 1980s the call was made for liberation before education. By the time of reassertion of community struggles and wider democratic objectives in the late 1980s, a more nuanced position included notions of using the boycott as a tactic and not an endless principle, the idea of liberation through education and the developing of education alternatives such as People's Education.

Where COSAS today has occasionally made 'militant' calls and taken students out of schools, it has seldom been for long periods and has not been politically and certainly not organisationally sustainable. In many ways, the struggle heritage of conflictual relations has been far less prevalent than a general lack of social or moral standards, of wandering around with little focus or academic purpose. Focus has been lost rather than been destructively applied.

Some of the strands of thinking and behaviour that were rooted in the struggle and the form it took are surely a useful topic for examination, despite the caveats and qualifications I have mentioned. I have started, however, with a plea not to be sweeping or simplistic and certainly to bring to the surface any lurking or hidden ideological or political assumptions or criticisms. Think about it before making sweeping generalisations, which say more about attitudes to the struggle than about root causes themselves.

The truly heroic impetus and sacrifices given by the children of 1976, and the way this drove forward the struggle for human rights and democracy in South Africa, should be an empathetic starting point for any discussion of problems. The moral and political dimensions of the struggle should not be forgotten, especially in a period where the fourth democratic elections are still quite fresh in people's minds.

Without the struggle and its successes, there would probably be little interest or reason for involvement in improving the educational results among black pupils anyway. The lack of skills certainly would not be influencing national economic growth in the way it does now. Black skills were never intended to be used. Now the skills shortage is on the agenda, and we are all involved.

One would expect that the generation that was most traumatised by the teargas, violent response, the deaths and beatings and throwing people in gaol, is precisely the parents today who are making these complaints about education. The struggle products of yesterday are today's parents who are most concerned about the state of their children's education and their attitude to learning. Many of the leaders of then are also the leaders of today, having further honed their skills of social organising through the 1980s period of wide and inclusive national struggles.

So is it their nostalgia and their difficulties in adjusting to the speed at which the world is changing, which are leading to complaint? It is really difficult to say how much the world has changed in its core values, whether moral compass and order have actually broken down and, if so, what has caused it. This complaint about indiscipline also has other causes than the heritage of student action. It is impossible in a short space to discuss the fast-changing realities of transformation, globalisation, technology, communication, and their social effects in the 21st century and the turbulent times through which we are currently living. Certainly, the culture of learning seems not to be deeply embedded among students. Some of this may well be because of learned responses and social breakdown in the struggle from the mid-1970s, but much of it may not.

There are some who argue that the current system is 'just like Bantu Education'. The SA Institute of Race Relations (SAIRR)[67] has said this and a leading black businesswoman has too. It is quite likely that such a statement is made without much thought, rather seeking to attract attention or at best to draw attention in a dramatic way to current real failings. I do not think such comparisons with a different system in a different context are very useful.

We do know that the outcomes today are terrible and we know that it is primarily poor, rural and township schools that perform the worst. But when someone like the businesswoman and many others today in leadership positions were at school through the 1970s and 1980s, there were probably only 20 000 students in secondary school in Soweto. A handful of sterling people nonetheless came through with flying colours. There were at different times great and well-respected teachers such as Wilkie Khambule or Es'kia Mphahlele or Curtis Nkondo, who should have been university professors, given their intellect.

More than that, under Bantu Education there was nowhere else for good middle-class people to go but teaching. Many teachers saw themselves as part of the liberation struggle through their efforts in raising the 'black child'. Today, of course, South Africa has nearly 600 000 children writing matric and close to 400 000 educators in all. The handful of sterling people who came through despite Bantu Education will surely also be reproduced today, but now in far greater numbers. Even in a bad system like today's there are more than a handful of bright, smart young people out there learning despite all the flaws.

Bantu Education, like apartheid, needed to be destroyed to create space for a new set of solutions and challenges to be faced. When a conservative organisation like the SAIRR draws the simplistic comparison with Bantu Education, it is doubtful they are calling for the flames of resistance to burn in the schools again. What sort of activism to change things are they suggesting?

If nothing else, a fundamental difference between those days and today is that now the government and its officials are, at least rhetorically, on the pupils' side, even if they are not quite getting it right. An activism under democracy would be significantly different from one opposing unequal Bantu Education, by allowing for the different context and a completely different role for the state today. Silly comparisons between today and the apartheid educational era, while drawing attention to some of the problems, are really only good for immediate political conversation and do not add much to the debate or help to focus on the real challenges we now face.

The teachers' scorecard

Perhaps more relevant in regard to the impact of the struggle is what has happened among the teachers, because it is in the classroom that we find the first level of the challenge to improve our children's education.

Teachers always appeared as a conflicted and even confused group in relation to the demands of the struggle. Loss of jobs and the challenge to authority had to be weighed against the pressures from students and the demands of communities from time to time. Middle-class aspirations and better prospects than the mass of the poor they taught, as well as some respect and influence in communities, would drive many teachers to stay on, no matter how frustrated they were. This despite the pressures of poor resources, administrative hierarchies, controls and difficult teaching conditions in many schools.

The 1980s and the extent of the involvement by different sectors in society impelled teachers to take a stand on a mass scale. Of course, many teachers simply love their children and their calling and are determined to do their best as committed professionals. Many teachers in the struggle years found themselves holding back within the professional imperatives of more moderate teacher unions. Others were disdainful of the multiclass and multisectoral struggles of organisations such as the UDF and NECC. Many teachers with this view were in unions such as the Teachers' League of SA – these were mainly 'coloured' teachers in the Western Cape, though they rejected all racial labels. They asserted 'old-fashioned' values of discipline and learning in arguing for education as a transformational force in itself.

White teachers were grouped in teacher organisations that emphasised professional values, were extremely hesitant about the struggle and were reluctant to get involved in politics. Many white teachers rejected the excesses of apartheid but found themselves in tightly controlled schools with an authoritarian education department that did not allow dissent. Some teachers did join the UDF as individuals or supported the white high-school organisations like the Pupils' Awareness and Action Group (PAAG) that tried to link with colleagues or comrades in the black schools. Rather than speaking out, liberal white teachers would mainly have expressed their opposition through the way they taught in the classroom, both in the explicit content and through getting their pupils to think independently, to challenge and not accept the system and its workings. Other white teacher bodies like the SAOU (SA Onderwysersunie) found themselves in direct support of apartheid education.

Black teachers found themselves caught directly in the front line between militant pupils and the authorities. The long-term results of the struggle years were far more likely to have been felt by and transmitted among teachers (and the education authorities) than among students. Perhaps it was the breaking of respect, the instability of dual pressures from above and below, a loss of authority in the classroom, lowering of respect in the eyes of the community: all of these factors would have influenced teachers' self-image. Teaching itself became less central and less obviously valued while students were on strike and political issues dominated the day.

The poor training of teachers and their ill-preparedness for new demands and new curricula, their failings in the realm of detailed pedagogies and methodologies of teaching, would obviously be less exposed in this period. Many of the dissatisfactions and pressures on teachers could be channelled into the new community and political movements, where teachers played an important role. New 'progressive' teachers' unions emerged throughout the country, eventually merging in the early 1990s into what was to be the SA Democratic Teachers' Union (SADTU), a strong union force in the wider trade union federation COSATU, and the largest public service union.

In 1990 and 1991 a Defiance Campaign in the schools, essentially led by the teachers, chased the last vestiges of the inspectorate out of schools. Inspectors were seen as an outside and hostile force, sent to intrude in schools and enforce unpopular authority.

It is likely that these moves, and this particular destruction of a relation of authority, were the strongest influences to be carried into the democratic period. Teachers thereafter fought tooth and nail to ensure that accountability systems and external controls on them were not enforced, coupling these with strong demands concerning pay and other labour relations issues. As the wider education movement (including students and parents) became demobilised in terms of direction and activities, with consequently less pressure on teachers, these more 'pure' union demands were to prevail over other developmental or educational goals.

The government's poor strategies in terms of engaging teachers and introducing new blood into the profession would only have reinforced this tendency and allowed teachers to cling to old habits and unspoken deficits in particular areas. An inefficient and inexperienced set of officials and administrative practices also reinforced teachers' perceptions that the departments could not be left with authority and discipline over a unified teaching corps. Departments themselves could not be entrusted to deliver on the things that would make the lives of teachers easier in terms of teaching. The job of the education department was thus likely to fall more and more into compliance mode – trying to enforce circulars and orders rather than assist teachers in a partnership.

Teachers faced a difficult situation. Apart from the backlogs in resources and capabilities, apart from the history of disorganisation and disorder in the running of the school, the government itself failed to come up with clear teacher training and development strategies. It never got right the training of new teachers, of ensuring there was enough new blood introduced into the system to ensure enthusiasm and new ways.

Tight 'manpower training' strategies tried to match needs with an exact supply of teachers. This meant that the approach to teacher training was not generous, but rather constrained and unsatisfactory. Where 20 000 teachers a year were required, 6 000 were produced by the teacher training institutions.

Teachers were in fact retrenched in 1996 and 1997, in an exercise meant to ensure teacher rationalisation and equalisation across race groups. Many of the more entrepreneurial and more experienced teachers took 'the package' and left the system. What this meant was further destabilisation of the profession and the loss of an older, more committed layer among teachers. Already there was an exodus into better-paid departmental jobs at national or provincial level.

Nonetheless, 120 teachers' training colleges, with a very mixed history of contribution to quality and excellence, were closed to allow for all teachers' training to happen in universities and as part of the wider merger of higher education going on at the time. The idea was to further professionalise education by making teachers study in the academic portals and halls of a university. In practice, it made it harder for rural children to access the calling, with expenses now including residences and the higher costs of higher education.

The decision to go this route has never really been satisfactorily explained or its implications and effects explored. The move has not in itself raised the professional capabilities of teachers. If it has led to new and expansive teacher training strategies, this has not been introduced into the discourse by government or the teacher training institutions themselves. I will say more about OBE and district development or support a little later, but for now suffice it to say that a history of poor collaboration between teachers and departmental officials has not been overcome.

We all know the difference a single good teacher can make. The evidence affirms the central role of teachers. At school, in class, the boundaries are set, and the techniques are inculcated for how to study, for methodologies and ways of achieving learning that is meaningful and relevant. The classroom, and the magic that happens at that coal-face of interaction between learner and teacher, is the starting point for all else that happens in education.

But there is evidence of low subject content knowledge on the part of many teachers. Especially in the fields of maths and science, this is hardly surprising. Teachers do not seem to be very good at planning, at phasing the work they have to teach, at deciding how to get through the important and core aspects of a year's work. While there is some blame placed on textbooks not always being available, this is probably exaggerated. Rather, teachers simply do not know how to use a textbook and are even less adept at knowing how to get students to engage with the books.

Evidence shows that in black schools especially, much time is often wasted. Out of a working week of 41 hours, on average 15.18 hours are spent on teaching (the remaining on administration, sports, form-filling and time-wasting activities), compared to 19.11 hours in former white schools, with less time in rural than urban areas as well.[68]

The basics of pedagogy are often absent. Certainly, at foundation levels, there is an absence of basic reading aloud, of continuous writing practice by learners, and use of techniques that would ensure that the foundations of literacy and numeracy can be put in place. This deficit bounces all the way up the system. It is not so much a problem of formal qualifications, because on the whole teachers have managed to upgrade at a formal level over the fifteen years of democracy. Rather, it is a lack of the core abilities to teach, even when the will is there.

Certainly, teaching has to be the only profession that is not subject to a formal system of accountability and monitoring. The Integrated Quality Management System (IQMS) has become an ongoing victim of poor and adversarial labour relations. The IQMS was an agreement reached in the Labour Relations Council in 2003, but that is still in 2009 the subject of discussion and finalisation. All sorts of structured and formal processes, from personal growth plans to staff development teams to school improvement plans have been formalised and their role defined. Most often, though, such good imperatives have just added to bureaucratic procedures and paperwork.

The introduction of a new curriculum statement in 2003 to replace the OBE-rooted Curriculum 2005 led to a flurry of courses and training schedules. Often these were no more than three days of orientation coupled with a cascading-down model to try and ensure replication. The new National Curriculum Statement (NCS) streamlined and simplified curricula into learning programmes with a continued emphasis on assessment throughout the year. The system put increased pressure and load on teachers.

The NCS and OBE have not fundamentally changed teachers' teaching practices, despite much confusion about OBE and a surprising degree of acceptance by many teachers. OBE allowed the good and child-centred teaching of the better schools to remain or be enhanced, while in the poorer schools it neither assisted nor turned around the poor quality of much teaching. It did somehow boost teachers' self-image through its focus on the empowered teacher as education leader and facilitator.

It finally reached the matric years with the Grade 12 class of 2008, variously described as 'guinea pigs' or as 'pioneers'. They in any case seemed to perform as well (or as badly) as in previous years, with a slight matric pass rate decline to 63%.[69]

Still, the existence of OBE has rather acted as a red herring for much confusion and complaint and an excuse for more elaborate jargon and form-filling. This has not necessarily contributed to a better quality of education. We know how widely OBE is blamed for a real frustration at difficulties in charting the course forward.

Another red herring is the elimination of corporal punishment. In our society, it is violence and abuse that are core problems. Even if one could beat pupils, there would still be a need to have a range of responses to ill discipline and a full repertoire of support and punishment. Violence could never be a first resort.

So the problem has to do with something else, something happening among pupils as well as teachers' lack of preparation for ways of dealing with this. It needs to be made clear that this is not confined to the poorer schools because various examples of bullying or corporal punishment in government schools in the suburbs have also come to light.

Teaching is a difficult and complex, multifaceted and multilayered art and science. Despite the shortfalls many teachers do much good work. I want to quote a heartfelt letter that was in the *Cape Times* on 23 February 2009. Vincent Hendricks from Elfindale in the Cape Flats points out that many teachers have been faithful to their teaching and their schools.

> I have been at my beloved Athlone High for 22 years and have enjoyed teaching English and geography to students for Grade 8 to Grade 12. I am sure I speak on behalf of thousands of good teachers who love their calling to teach, and everything that goes with the vocation – the diligent preparation, dynamic lessons, setting up tests and assignments, marking of papers and sports coaching, to mention but a few areas . . .

He goes on to say that teachers are expected to be 'policemen, sexologists, criminologists, psychologists, drug counsellors, doctors, nurses, sports coaches, tour guides, peace-makers, pastors, fundraisers for the state' and, of course, to do their primary job of teaching – 'or is that to assess or be a filing clerk?' he asks. No wonder he is angry; he earns a gross salary of R13 888 per month. He asks about the high student/teacher ratio, talks about the teacher 'retrenchments' and their impact, and complains about student discipline.

Reasons for some of the learners' errant behaviour are dynamic and complex. These include abuse in certain homes and in the community, and behaviour at home that is violent, crude and sexual. There is a general lawlessness in our society. Certain politicians, pop stars and sports stars are poor role models for our children. Some learners come to school with lots of attitude. Can the teachers change the behaviour of all the children? Education and good manners begin in the home.

He ends by pleading with the public not to generalise about teachers. 'There are many good teachers left in the profession and we are doing a sterling job. It will be nice to hear something positive about teachers.' He is right; you cannot keep beating down on a profession and expect it to produce of its best, to feel inspired to take on critical tasks and ask questions of itself, its goals and its practices.

Yet if we do not get it right – in the classrooms, with teachers, in the schools and districts where support should be paramount, and in the society where so many of the problems are located – we are simply reinforcing the inequalities of our society, and smashing the hopes and dreams of the new post-democratic generation that rightly expects to be given access to the possibilities and real aspirations of the world today. Efforts should surely smooth the way, not create roadblocks and obstacles.

Many teachers have low morale and would love to get out of the profession. Over half want to leave.[70] A national strike in 2007 bore witness to levels of frustration. Teachers have many complaints, none of which can be ignored or do not have their roots in some aspect of reality. Salaries for teachers are too low; classes are overcrowded; resources are not up to scratch, whether toilets, laboratories or libraries.

As I indicated in Chapter 3, the physical aspects of some schools, including staff rooms for teachers, leave a lot to be desired. In addition, many teachers cannot get a housing subsidy outside the bigger centres of a province or are reluctant to build or purchase in a small rural village. Others catch taxis daily, say from Mthatha or Mafikeng, to outlying and surrounding rural villages. Again, it is not surprising that they often arrive late or leave early, or as soon as their school day allows.

None of this lets the departments or officials off the hook. Districts should be the site of extensive political and curriculum support for teachers, yet are often the location for a 'compliance' mentality and a surplus of form-filling and other anti-educational rituals and behaviours.

What kind of teacher leadership does one find in response to these challenges?

Teacher unions: labour trumps education

One of the greatest silences in education today is discussion on the role of the unions. No doubt COSATU is a central part of the ANC-led Tripartite Alliance; no doubt workers in a capitalist economy deserve protection, especially a Wild West world economy in crisis. No one disputes the realities of labour relations and grievances of teachers. But why are we so scared to discuss the role of teacher unions in a constructive, supportive, but critical way? The negative aspects of the role of unions can be summarised in the example of one particular union official.

Ronald Nyathi – spokesman for SADTU and a senior official in Gauteng province – was responding to the decision by the SA Council for Educators (SACE) to name and shame teachers who abuse children at school and are convicted of this. Child abuse is a scourge in our society. Teachers who have sexual relations with their learners have no place in our schools, in fact should be in gaol. Yet Nyathi found it in himself to defend such teachers. Firstly, he blamed the Department of Education for not running enough 'workshops to train the teachers'. Secondly, he said naming teachers was unacceptable because it would 'ruin their careers' and they would find it impossible to get employment in the future.[71] He just does not get it.

He had done this before. When learners in Alexandra complained about teachers not turning up in class and about child abuse, Nyathi led the Alexandra teachers on strike. He threatened students with 'extreme violence' if they came to school and vowed never to listen to learners, the department or the concerned parents. 'We are professionals,' he said, 'and professionals only listen to their peers.' When asked if this was morally acceptable, he told *Business Day* he did not know about morals but it was politically effective.[72]

In 2008, a circular was sent to SADTU members in Gauteng, warning teachers not to participate in 'unauthorised' Saturday or out-of-hours programmes, especially with the department, whether cultural programmes or AIDS-support training. If they did, disruptions and violence would be the order of the day, the circular threatened.[73]

A few months later Nyathi was at it again. This time, he went head to head with Minister of Education Naledi Pandor and the ANC, claiming that there would never be stability in schools till Jacob Zuma was elected president,[74] and stating that teachers would hold political meetings in school time if they needed to.[75] Union leadership is unable publicly to draw a line and to assert effective control over antisocial remarks made by its officials.

Finally, the education departments remain a soft target, with many complaints rooted in truth about inefficiency and poor delivery. Even where teacher unions have signed into common campaigns with the department, like the Quality Learning and Teaching Campaign, they nonetheless often cannot hold themselves back from putting blame on the government rather than taking responsibility for areas they may be able to fix.

This is classic victim behaviour. 'We did not have enough workshops to know that child abuse was unacceptable' is obviously an extreme example of such victim mentality. Are we going to forever throw up our hands and behave as perpetual victims? This is what we inherited – how do we all take responsibility, in our spheres and where we are? Yes, it includes complaining, organising and fixing things that are seen not to be working. But it involves a constructive perspective on change and our own role in making that change.

The Polokwane resolutions of the ANC and subsequent campaigns, including their 2009 election manifesto, were absolutely right, then, to put teachers at the heart of the education recovery so that teaching could be restored to the noble profession it should be.[76] This can only happen for teachers if we as a society can value learning and achievement, for learning is a social goal and not just something restricted to teachers.

And 'teachers shall be in class, on time, teaching', no ifs or buts.[77] This is the least parents and learners, society in general, expect from teachers (and the officials too) – that they do their job, especially in a 'developmental' state where even more is expected of government. Both department and teachers are in this together. Problems in one area do not let officials or stakeholders off the hook in another.

The Education Roadmap (see Chapter 6) compiled by the Development Bank of Southern Africa with education department officials and teacher unions, as well as the ANC, devotes 40% of its ten-point programme to teachers. There are the injunctions about being in class, on time, teaching, and using textbooks. But also there are ways of encouraging new blood, of creating enthusiasm and career paths for new graduates entering the profession, through bursaries, better pay, and even a sense of excitement and duty. Then the Roadmap talks extensively about teacher development, about how to support and train teachers in the field, and about the role of teacher unions in addressing this.

I think it would not be amiss to say to teachers that they risk squandering much of the goodwill of the public if all the public sees is negative behaviour and complaint. There are many parents and educationists ready to lynch teachers, figuratively speaking. The public, and also teachers as a whole, do not hear aloud the parallel discourse of development; that side is drowned out by the labour relations complaints of the teacher unions, however legitimate. The public does not hear how teachers are going to contribute and does not see the programmes to help teachers share resources and ideas or develop coping strategies. No doubt the work is there – but it is hidden as a subordinate discourse and it takes a poor second place.

What happened to the democratic teachers' unions of the 1980s, who could not be silenced from their concerns and debates round People's Education? Fighting for immediate rights and benefits of teachers seems to have taken precedence over questions of their social role and contribution to development. Labour trumps development every time.

How do the thousands of teachers Vincent Hendricks spoke about in his letter, who do their jobs and love their children, find a voice and a platform to be appreciated, challenged and cajoled? It is to be hoped that the all-in teacher summits on development that have been planned will produce a shift in attitudes and priority.

Around 400 000 teachers have the lives and futures of twelve million children entrusted to them almost every day. It is an enormous task. Such a huge responsibility asks of society to acknowledge the debt it owes to teachers and the nobility of a profession from whom such high outputs are required.

Someone to lean on

Ultimately, the state must take responsibility for the situation in government or public schools. Less than 3–5% of children are in private or independent schools. Maybe 10% are in ex-model-C schools.[78] So the primary job of government is to attend to the mass of pupils who find themselves in non-performing township and rural schools, pupils from the poorer schools, whose poor education reinforces their desperate status of exclusion and marginalisation in a democratic country.

Government has to support schools with efficient service delivery – the second level of importance in the toxic mix that has led to failure. While we have looked to the history and the sociology of the transition to try and understand the context and structures that shaped people, we have to assess the active interventions of government as a crucial ingredient.

Government bureaucracy is primarily about providing the management and administrative order for an effective school system, the resources, from buildings to textbooks, and the pedagogical and institutional supports that would enable a trained and ready teaching force to teach in the classroom and take its wards through an adequate curriculum that meets their needs and those of the country.

However well intentioned, has government begun to address the backlogs and to set the country on the road to a quality education system? The record is mixed, with positive and negative features, but on balance we will have to say that government has not been getting it right.

One of the most important blockages to effective delivery is constitutional. The constitution defines education delivery as a provincial competence at the schools' level. I am not against decentralisation and local choice. Many solutions need to be carefully crafted to meet very specific situations in individual schools, so one-size-fits-all approaches are often ineffective. There is little evidence that this flexibility is advanced through our constitutional dispensation, which puts policy development in the hands of national government but decentralises aspects of schools' delivery to the provinces.

Decentralisation means there is a layer of politicians between national outlooks and local implementation. It also means substantial places to hide from direct accountability and the ability to shift blame continually. It is unclear where responsibility lies.

The constitution makes it enormously difficult to shift resources across regions, human or otherwise, in an innovative, rational and flexible way. Follow the money and the provincial funding formulae take over. It is hard to move support teams from province to province. It is hard to insist that solutions from one area be applied more broadly. Once the budgets are transferred to the provincial treasury and are subject to provincial shaping and design, the national education department cannot even insist that monies allocated from the national treasury for education are actually spent on schooling rather than, say, welfare shortfalls. A load of vested interests and localised corruptions may occur.

Today, of course, there are ten education departments (one national and nine provincial) that have replaced the fourteen racially based education departments of the past. The problems are different but some of the administrative difficulties are written into the system's very structure.

None of this is an in-principle argument for national control, which also has significant downsides. As with OBE, there might well be individual teachers, schools or provinces that can rise to the challenge of more complex systems. For the majority of provinces, however, provincialisation does not seem to have led to significant local choice or improvement.

The changes in the number of political heads or MECs in the Eastern Cape, and the large number of acting heads of the department there, with enormous negative consequences, only show up the most extreme example of the difficulties of the national government to intervene in a meaningful way. Even where education appears almost to take on the features of a failed state, it is difficult to invoke the constitutional provisions that would allow decisive interference by the national government. Despite poor audits, underspending, corruption that includes hundreds of millions stolen from school nutrition programmes (and few charges or convictions), the Eastern Cape continues to deny most of its rural students the possibility of a better life through a meaningful education. Up to now, the national government has been able to do little but talk about standards and policy implementation.

The other significant place where government has not performed is at the district level. The education district provides services to a cluster of schools and is probably the best place to organise administration, support and curriculum advice, as well as supervision. For a range of reasons from vacancies and inexperienced staffing to inadequate prioritisation, districts have not functioned on a large scale as sites of support to schools.

Often they have been the source of paperwork and compliance control, trying to assert authority rather than win respect through the useful exercise of genuine authority in relevant teaching areas. Where the provincial roadblock is something we may simply have to acknowledge and work with or work around, the school districts remain significant sites of intervention where real gains can be made in the quality of support to schools.

The management responsibilities of the principal are enormous and often crucial to the functioning or non-functioning of a school. This letter written by Tom Clarke, headmaster at Parktown Boys, is as informative as the letter written by a teacher that I quoted earlier. The principal argues that the management structure at a school should be reviewed in order to manage the school more effectively.

> The outdated practice of giving all the accountability for management and organisation to the principal needs to be addressed. Management of schools needs to refocus on these areas: curriculum (subjects, timetables, teacher requirements, subject choice), assessment practices (continuous assessment, portfolios, projects, tests, exams), extra-curricular (culture, sport, leadership, character development), resources (equipment, books, teaching aids), computer administration and e-learning, discipline and student affairs (codes of conduct, grade heads, houses, disciplinary hearings), counselling (interviews, therapy, motivation), public relations with the community, personnel and HR for both educators and service staff (salaries, conditions of service, appointments, staff morale), budgeting and financial controls of income and expenditure (school fee issues, exemptions, financial accountability), grounds and building maintenance (safety, security, renovation, development), registration and admissions.
>
> The principal, as the department representative, should be responsible for the overall leadership of the above, but cannot possibly cope with all these responsibilities alone.[79]

Whatever the details of the solutions, there has to be a sophisticated range of responses at the departmental level to ensure that principals are in place and can attend to the enormity of their tasks. With a total of 26 000 public schools, it is not surprising that the leadership required to achieve these tasks would not spontaneously exist in all cases or appear in a democratic dispensation simply by wishing for it.

Some of government's larger failures were due to overoptimistic understandings of education and the acceptance of advice from progressive, well-meaning advisors with little grounded tradition in government or policy-making at the level of the state. Advisors linked to the ANC, especially academics and researchers, would have come from a tradition of dissidence in largely English-language universities. They often have overromanticised the capacities and realities on the ground.

The National Education Policy Initiative (NEPI) investigation of 1991–2 essentially drew together the collective wisdom of progressive academic educationists and provided much of the base for later policy choices under a democratic government. It needs to be revisited to see how realistic their recommendations were and to understand these in their context.

Romantic notions were carried forward from the struggle days, translated into superficial administrative systems with dire consequences. The mobilisation of parents was to be accomplished through the universal acceptance of school governing bodies as a natural follow-on from community involvement in education during the struggle years.

Yet the updated approach was often bureaucratic and formalistic, and it limited education options rather than expanding assistance to schools. It might mean community insistence that outsiders not be employed, or defensive and conservative positions to prevent demographic changes or sharing of resources in better-off schools. Current power relations in a community were not addressed, so that populist and intimidatory elements might assert themselves. Middle-class parents and middle-class schools might be better resourced to achieve certain aims.

And of course there are situations where the involvement of parents really muddles clarity in a school. In a recent example of bullying at a public boys' school, it was often parents who spoke out in support of 'initiation' practices and maintaining the traditions of the school, labelling the bullied child as the social problem. The role and responsibilities of the principal as leader often and in so many ways become fudged. So, rather than creating more social resources and networks, romanticised notions of popular involvement did not always translate into better conditions and order in the schools.

OBE was one of the casualties that emerged from these policy deficiencies. It was necessary to rewrite the syllabi that apartheid had passed down, and also to create a common learning experience for all young South Africans attuned to the changing modern world. This should be child-centred and critical, creative, innovative, shaped to a technological world – as OBE was.

But while OBE never intended to stop proper learning of basic skills in literacy and numeracy, it allowed a shallow view of empowerment and active educational engagement to take root. This was an approach that might have been challenging in well-resourced schools with teachers confident in their subject knowledge, in their classroom pedagogies and understanding of how to engage the kids before them. It was certainly not going to work well in schools where pedagogies were already poor and resources limited.

Obviously any new system would take time to embed, so teething problems should not be overexaggerated. Nonetheless, it is quite true that the training and supports for the introduction of OBE were insufficient. By the time of the revision of Curriculum 2005 and the design of the National Curriculum Statement, there was already a realisation that strong emphasis would nonetheless have to be placed on the foundations of learning.

Another of these overoptimistic, overelaborate schemes was found in the setting up of the rather complicated qualifications and skills training institutions. The SAQA (South African Qualifications Authority) and SETA (Sector Education and Training Authority) systems combined a complex and difficult definition of unit standards to be attained in education and training with a decidedly bureaucratic and mechanical architecture. Genuine educational establishments would have to wade through this. Rather than emphasising support in a way that builds capabilities and delivery on the ground, a set of high-level stumbling blocks would be put in place. The unit standards developed in any case had a fixed and fragmented underlying theory of knowledge and learning that is actually quite old-fashioned.

Such elaborate schemes fell into place, then, due to bad and abstract policy advice, often out of touch, in this case uncritically drawing on unworkable proposals from New Zealand and Australia. While the ideas did not really even work on paper they allowed for a lot of 'policy posturing' about portability and recognition of prior learning that had popular appeal. They were overoptimistic and out of context, and they put emphasis in entirely the wrong direction – a bureaucratic and controlled approach rather than an empowering, supportive framework. Now it is hard to find the boldness to do away with such policy mistakes and suggest a different beginning.

Jonathan Jansen, educationist and vice-chancellor of the University of the Free State, has argued the natural tendency of government to engage in what he calls 'political symbolism'[80] or what I call 'policy posturing'. Where there are complex problems, simple solutions are found and presented as the be-all and end-all. The orientation programmes of OBE that were presented as comprehensive training are one such example. The R1.9 billion or more spent on recapitalising the FET vocational colleges is another. The expenditure was presented as if this would save vocational education.

Off the agenda fell the basic question as to whether the amount was faintly sufficient. With this problem 'solved', no real attention was transferred to the problems of training, retaining skilled staff, resourcing the technical and field workshops or managing the institutions either. As practical questions they keep appearing, of course. Now, as a range of significant other and new problems emerge, policy continues to muddle through while the devastating fundamental deficiencies have disappeared from public discourse. Unintended consequences and emerging complexities are usually edited out in favour of a narrative of constant, upward progress.

Two other examples of this kind of 'posturing' are the moves around fee-free schools and calls for free education (sometimes including up to tertiary). I do not want to address the importance and value of saving a certain amount in the pockets of poor parents through fee elimination. In fact, I strongly support it. These calls arise from a fundamentally good understanding of how socio-economic status and poverty impact on schooling.

I do not want to address the need to go beyond rhetoric to understand what free schooling would mean, its costs and the requirements for its implementation. I am not going to ask in detail why the small and new elite with university degrees should not have to pay back loans and government subsidies to ensure viable education for incoming streams.

All I want to point to is how issues such as fee-free schools become symbolic, enabling government to claim it is on course to deal with poverty. Meanwhile, the range of other problems is not adequately addressed, whether to do with improving schools (paying them on time, helping them to ensure access while not threatening the viability of model-Cs) or to do with other poverty impacts: from school uniforms, hunger and disease to the issue of why poor children face such low-quality education. A policy such as fee-free schools enables a blanket claim to be made that the issues of poverty are being addressed, perhaps to the detriment of asking more difficult questions.

An active citizenry is necessary to hold government to less defensive positions, to get it to admit to faults, and to help it to design programmes that will have an impact in appropriately complex ways at the appropriate levels and in the right coordinated mix. Left alone, government does not spontaneously acknowledge problems or admit difficulties; it tends to defend its actions at all costs. If citizens fold their arms and leave things up to the state, the slow pace of advance will never be sufficient to put South Africa on the right road.

Even the most well-meaning civil servants can quickly become blasé and inappropriately disengaging and limited in relation to their 'clientele', the public. This happens all over the world. Perhaps, too, in

South Africa we need to understand problems of delivery in education in relation to the broader problems of delivery in government as a whole, and as a subset of the difficulties government has had up to now of developing accountability and responsibility systems with bite.

This makes education both a special challenge and a hopeful beneficiary of the new administration's commitment to an efficient 'developmental state'[81] and to service that benefits poor and working-class constituencies in the first instance.

There are too many tales of salaries not being paid by departments, of strikes being unfairly monitored by officials, of transport for poor scholars not being in place, of corruption and theft, of non-transference of moneys to fee-free schools, and so on. The disappearance of millions in school nutrition money in the Eastern Cape is the most extreme and perhaps the most shocking example, but it is not entirely unrepresentative.

Accountability systems, monitoring, and reward and punishment are for departmental officials as much as for teachers. Professional behaviour is essential for civil servants, whether they are teachers in the classroom or those who manage the school supports that ensure the ability to teach effectively. We need to find ways to encourage and reward good performance in the classroom and in terms of the official support to schools – ways to gently hold the feet of both civil servants/officials and teachers to the fire.

The OECD has a nicely balanced take on the challenges of the transition, pointing out that since 1994, debates on the effectiveness of education policies have largely turned on whether they are ambitious or practical enough.

> On the one hand, it might be argued that, in the context of post-Apartheid reconciliation, policy formulation was constrained by the political compromises made . . . the effects of which were to protect both existing white and emerging black middle-class interests. On the other hand, it can be said that policy implementation has simply been checked and delayed by the depth

and extent of Apartheid under-education, coupled with a current lack of managerial capacity and a limited budget. A third position might be that rapid, visible and collective formulation of what have often been highly advanced and idealistic, even revolutionary, education policies has had important political and symbolic effects in itself, despite the sluggishness of actual policy implementation, and especially amidst popular expectations of substantial – and not only educational – social transformation.[82]

The OECD goes on to say that the reform ideas were 'of a high conceptual quality', but that change management, or transformational leadership, failed.

Successful change requires more than new structures and processes, technology or policy; in particular, it requires the engagement and participation of the people affected by the change, and a new set of behaviours and values. In the course of its field visits, the team could see and hear that some reforms did not reach (or really influence) schools and classrooms. It is also clear that the capacity of some provincial departments and of school leaders to manage change and introduce reforms should be improved.[83]

Lastly, in this section I want to say a few words on the particular style of successive ministers of education under democracy. All of them had strengths, but their flaws leave the door wide open to making some sweeping statements about these primary failures as well. Sometimes, of course, their very strengths were the source of their major weaknesses.

It is hard to assess a particular leadership heritage. This task is always contradictory and needs balance. Nonetheless, none of the ministers of education has been able to set South Africa on the road to recovery. As they are the responsible political figures, one hopes that the buck stops with them, with all the failures they have left behind.

The first education minister, Sibusiso Bengu, was an affable and academically competent man. His task was to totally reorientate the education system and set in place new systems and administrative processes, as well as pass and implement a new Schools Act. He was ponderous and methodical. His director-general (DG) too was not going to be hurried and would slowly marshal the technical expertise. Yet, as we have seen, this was also a period of overoptimistic and abstract policy advice. There was a bureaucratic channelling combined with unrealistic and overelaborate policy requirements.

The means were never set in place to achieve the high-sounding goals. More than that, and certainly more concerning, is that under Minister Bengu's stewardship the impetus and interest in education as transformation was slowly allowed to dissipate. As with demobilisation of energy and involvement throughout the society as a whole, so with the education movement specifically. Its former vibrancy became more fragmented, less committed. It was less clear in its goals. This would contribute even more to a general retreat into technicism, dependence on 'experts' who did not engage widely, and slow solutions presented as energetic response.

Meanwhile, the matric results faltered and started to decline, along with education expenditure as GEAR started to bite. Minister Kader Asmal arrived in 1999 with a strong mandate to take the bit between his teeth. Matric pass rates had dropped to 47% in 1997 and 49% in 1999.[84]

His was a style completely opposite to that of the previous incumbent. Where Bengu was polite and moderate, almost self-effacing, Asmal was bombastic and sure of his opinions and views. He was known for publicly flailing his officials and giving them embarrassing dressing-downs. He introduced an honesty about results and a public acknowledgement of the deficiencies and even continuities with the poor results of the past. His solution was endless energy, new definitions and new programmes and commitments.

As one set of commentators said at the time, Asmal's statement of priorities on 27 July 1999 and the call to revitalise the country's education and training system generally drew favourable comment.

> The Minister's statement represents an honest and open appraisal, and presents a vision of education transformation which prioritises the key areas of education requiring urgent attention. The general interest cannot be attributed solely to the highly visible media presence of the Minister, conjuring up as it does the image of a very energetic leader determined to sweep aside the supposed inertia of the last five years. Nor is the interest generated because of anything new in the Minister's statement. Most of the priorities identified by the Minister were the very ones which sustained the pre-1994 struggles, on the crest of which the democratic government took office.[85]

Asmal successfully oversaw an improvement in matric pass rates, though there were criticisms about the early dropout it might have implied. By 2004 the rate was back up to 71% (slowly dropping to the mid to low 60s by 2008).[86] Yet, no system could base itself on the individual energy and storm cloud of electricity created by an individual. The DG struggled to keep up and as a result created an administrative and systemic mess.

By the time Asmal retired and the DG had been moved to cooperate in equally disconnected style with the eccentric minister of health, it was too late. Any gains there might have been were not institutionalised or bedded down. Without systems and institutionalised processes, the new visions remained like clouds obscuring the view and with some disruptive effect.

Recognising this and dealing with the administrative backlog was one of the strengths of the third minister, Naledi Pandor. Her DG was a former unionist himself and understood the need for routine and functioning bureaucracies. There was much improvement in basic administration, such as delivery of textbooks, extension of the school nutrition scheme, and the logistical success of running timeous and consistent national matric exams, with the whole host of backroom functions this implied.

To their credit, the minister and DG gave a sense of stabilising the education system, of battening down policy resolutions and attempting to begin to address them in a systematic way, of getting down to doing the job without dramatics or histrionics.

If there is one serious criticism, it is that all this technical focus was nonetheless too technicist. By this I mean that slow bureaucratic advance became confused with success. Processes were too internal-looking; the reference point was in thick documents with targets rather than in the vague and woolly world of the aspirations of the public at large.

Administrative logic explained decisions rather than there being a conversation with an engaged social network. Critique and academic interaction were often seen as an irritant. This went with an inability to draw in the extensive body of education participants outside of the state. People outside of the state, but involved in a range of educational work, did not know how to connect and contribute even where they felt they had something to offer.

While Pandor did speak to business or to NGOs, she had a school-marm's top-down frame of reference that left the education world less empowered. In a period where the education faults and non-delivery were becoming more glaring and discussed in public, where demands grew higher, it was crucial that the education department did not lose touch with this energy. Yet the minister failed to engage, and hence doomed even herself to fail.

Step by step, moderate improvements, without a network and architecture of support, were not sustained but continually slipped back in one arena as they advanced in another. Why should society wait forever, especially in the absence of visible answers beyond the 'trust us' variety? More than that, Pandor failed to release the energies and skills of organisations and citizens ready to contribute.

Education had to become more 'political'. The critique that emerged at the ANC's 2007 Polokwane conference, the suggestion that education needed to become a wider social concern, seemed to understand the dangers of an inherently depoliticised and desocialised view of education change.

It is fair to say that the average minister coming to power in one of the mature democracies might set one or two clear goals and define a couple of pet areas for intervention. In a five-year term, he or she would be expected to make an impact but not to turn a system around. Much evidence and international experience show how hard it is to define improvements in outcomes as the central goal and then to achieve this, especially in a term or two.

Yet here in South Africa, incoming ministers were expected to recreate the bureaucracy, design and staff the institutions, inspire and organise the educational participants – and do all of this in a way that fundamentally altered the access, success and outcomes levels of all young people. Did we not all expect too much from the transition, hoping that change would come in one centralised policy bundle rather than seasons of bite-sized chunks, of pieces of progress, of slow advance within an overall direction and goalposts that would continually shift?

Such considerations must be part of the story when we seek to blame participants, when we demand more and call for better targeted and better implemented programmes that work.

We can see the toxic mix that threatens to lock us in a cycle of doomed despair. History and its inheritance, the structures of inequality, the attitudes and deficits passed down, are added to the actions and the choices of those who govern and those who are paid to teach. Poor administration and unsatisfactory teaching are not just structural issues, but the results of conscious choice and the way we have organised ourselves and our institutions to perfom their tasks. Leadership means precisely calling leaders to account.

There are now two education ministries, allowing government to focus in a dedicated way on basic education (schooling) and on higher education and technical/vocational training. The new minister of basic education, Angie Motshekga, was formerly an MEC in Gauteng where she was political head of the provincial education department. Here she had opportunity to stare down some of the worst excesses of the teachers' unions. In one case, she appealed straight to Soweto parents rather than allow teachers to refuse administrative controls, calling on them to 'rise up' against the antisocial behaviours exhibited. She is also head of the ANC Women's League, which will enhance her reach into communities and her ability to mobilise people around education concerns. On these counts, there is much positive about her appointment as the political minister responsible for schooling and finding ways to fix it.

Clearly, there are lots of issues to be put on the table, lots of complexities to discuss. We will look a little later in this chapter at the many achievements of the education system under democracy. For now, perhaps we should not get too complex. The answers in the end require simplicity: clear priorities, agreed goals and targets. It is not too simple to demand an enthusiasm that says 'Let's just do it!' and stop all this messing around.

The social price of poverty

Whereas teachers in the classroom are the first level of influence on the outcomes of education and support to the schools is the second, the third level is the wider society. Many of the problems that have an impact on education are not caused by anything that happens in schools, but brought from society into the classroom. At this third level, wider coordination and broader social solutions will be needed to address the causes of poor performance.

For a range of reasons that I explored in Chapter 3, many students do not enter the classroom in a state that has prepared them to learn. Whether through educational deficits or social dynamics that hamper learning, poorer students are at a serious disadvantage. Blame lies, if anywhere, in broader social policy and its inadequacies and challenges.

In relation to the children, such inadequacy is unforgivable. Education is just one of the challenges they face. As we saw in the previous chapter, the effects of unemployment and poverty are devastating. Remember too that these children often face a lack of learning support in the home, sexual violence and inappropriate sexual relations in the classroom, added responsibilities when parents die of AIDS, and peer pressure to take drugs or to drink. Crime and gang-related violence within the community also affect learners in a host of negative ways.

All this, then, is their social capital. The differing social capital of poor and rich children is one of the strongest reasons for inequalities and relatively weak outcomes in poor communities and schools. At every turn, the networks, assets, capabilities and social capital available to poor communities are subject to stress and pressure leading to their ongoing exclusion. The cycle of exclusion and marginalisation is reproduced and deepened through the schooling system itself, with the most negative effects on poor schools and pupils who can least afford it.

In the face of this, it is apparent why children need the school. It can be a place of refuge, one space with order, a set of caring frameworks that encourages them to become what they want to be. This may be academic learning, or it may be to become a sports hero or to develop a musical talent.

Without a space in which our youngsters can learn and grow, we stagnate as a nation. Without getting our schools right, without creating these nurturing boundaries of support and care, we betray the generations of the future. They will sink into the morass. We will all be to blame unless there is the sky for them to grasp.

What government has done right

Apart from what still needs to be done, it is imperative that we understand what has already been achieved in a fairly short space of time. Twelve million of our children are in school today. Virtually all of the primary-age children are actually in school, with equal numbers of girls and boys. On both key counts, we have met the Millennium Development Goals set by the United Nations in September 2000.

Further significant achievements include the amalgamation and unification of the various apartheid education systems and Bantustan establishments into a single national department responsible for broad policy, and the provincial establishments responsible for delivery.

The SA Schools Act of 1996 laid the basis for a non-racial approach to education with common perspectives for all. There were strides towards equalising expenditure across the racial divides and in relation to provincial inequalities, as well as dealing with issues such as size of classes, access to teachers and course materials, and so on, through the new Norms and Standards, which saw increasing pro-poor expenditure. Budgets shifted significantly in favour of poorer provinces, with a reduction in inequality of some 60% by 2001.[87]

This has been followed by a raft of policy papers, reports, legislation, implementation directives and institutional development that shows progress across many branches of education, from higher to vocational.

Within the fiscal landscape – and despite the strictures of GEAR – there has been a massive emphasis on education. At its height some 6% of GDP and approximately 21% of the national budget was allocated to education, sinking around the GEAR period and rising again in real terms more recently to about 5% of GDP.[88]

South Africa's spend on education is substantial. Clearly, there is room for more money. But the problem does not seem to be too little money in the first place, but rather the use of this money. Organisation and efficient administration would be more important than simply increasing the amount of resources: it is making sure such resources are used to achieve desirable outcomes that is the issue. In fact, South African education is not creating 'bang for the buck', given the large amounts spent on education.

In 2008 there were over twelve million students in public and independent schools, with 385 860 educators in the 26 269 schools. In 2003, there were some twelve million learners, 26 845 ordinary schools, 362 598 educators and a budget of R69.1 billion. By 2004/5, education expenditure was R76.6 billion. By the 2007/8 budget, with Finance

Minister Trevor Manuel's call to step up education outcomes, education was accounting for R105.5 billion of government spending (welfare coming in second at R89.4 billion). The education pie in real monetary terms was 49% larger in 2005 than it was in 1994.[89]

The syllabus has had to be redesigned and rewritten for the democratic scenario, underlaid by the progressivist assumptions of OBE with its learner-based and critical teaching strategies as initially laid out in Curriculum 2005.

At the outcomes level, a strong focus by the second education minister, Kader Asmal, saw matric results improve from a poor 58% pass rate in 1994 and worse 47% in 1997, to 73% in 2003. This fell to 71% in 2004, 67% in 2006 and 63% by the time the first OBE generation wrote matric in 2008.

Looking at the matric results:

- 495 408 wrote in 1994; 18% gained matric exemption/endorsement, which allows access to university
- 552 384 wrote in 1998; only 49% passed, just 12% with endorsement
- 440 096 wrote in 2003; 55% passed, 19% with endorsement
- 508 363 wrote in 2005; 347 184 passed to give a 68% pass rate, 17% with endorsement
- 528 525 wrote in 2006; 352 078 passed to give a 67% pass rate, 16% with endorsement
- 564 775 wrote in 2007; 368 217 passed to give a 65% pass rate, 15% with endorsement
- 589 912 candidates sat for the 2008 examination, based on the National Curriculum Statement, but the results of only 533 561 candidates were announced;[90] 333 681 passed to give a 63% pass rate, 20% with endorsement.[91]

The number of students passing maths and science on higher grade has improved only marginally over the years. In 2006, only 25 217 passed matric maths on a higher grade (317 642 wrote maths and

165 865 passed, including higher and lower grades).[92] But fewer than 3% of matrics got a pass good enough to give them access to university courses such as engineering or accounting requiring higher grade. It is too early to call the meaning of an apparent increase in numbers passing mathematics under the new matriculation dispensation, which has also abolished the higher grade/standard grade distinction.

A disappointment has been the falling rate of matric exemptions, from just around 17% to 15%. While 82 010 attained endorsement in 2003 and 86 531 in 2005, this was still fewer than the 88 497 back in 1994. In 2008 the matric exemption rate rose to 20%, meaning the numbers gaining university exemption did increase to 107 462.[93]

The slow general progress in access has meant a steady increase in the average educational attainment of the population. Between 2002 and 2007, the percentage of individuals with no education decreased from 12% to 9%; the percentage of those who completed Grade 12 (matric) increased from 21% to just under 24%; and the percentage of those with more than a primary education increased from 64% to 70%.[94]

There have been dramatic institutional changes in the higher education and FET college landscape. For instance, 120 teacher training colleges have been merged into university education departments in an attempt to improve quality and critical approaches. In addition, the higher education scene has seen 36 institutions merged into 21 universities and universities of technology, and some 150 FET colleges reduced to 50 through the 1998 FET Act. The 2006 revisions to the FET Act prepared for a new era of emphasis on vocational skills and training.

Black student enrolment at universities and technikons grew from 191 000 in 1993 to 343 000 in 1999, and 449 000 in 2003. Including distance learning, the figure was up to 741 383 in 2006. Black students made up 59% of the university headcount in 1999 and 64% in 2003, the figure being 86% for technikons; 53% were women.[95]

The National Student Financial Aid Scheme (NSFAS) was a R70 million scheme in 1994, with around 28 000 beneficiaries. By 2004 it was worth R985 million, with some 114 000 beneficiaries, and has now expanded to two billion Rand.

It does have to be said that higher education institutions currently have pretty awful pass rates too. Only 30% of students of all races had graduated after five years, with 66% of students at former technikons not graduating. Whereas 65% of white students studying language degrees graduate within five years, only 26% of black students do. In business and management studies, the ratio is 83:33. More stark than the throughput, though, is that 60% of young whites actually begin a tertiary education, as opposed to only 12% of African and coloured youth.[96]

What these figures show is that there are still massive challenges of transformation. Nonetheless, there is clearly also a positive continuity in the school and wider education system. There are important levels of stabilisation and delivery and there is a cohort of students who are managing to attain high levels of achievement.

It is also clear that government is aware of significant problems and has put important programmes in place to address some of these. Some of these programmes include:

- the school nutrition programme, which in 2006 provided meals to 6.05 million learners in 18 039 schools nationally
- the Dinaledi programme to identify specific schools where a focus on mathematics and technology excellence could be developed, reaching over 400 schools in 2008 and with some signs of improving mathematics pass rates
- bursaries and incentives to enter teacher training, encouraging an increase in enrolment seen at the beginning of 2008
- improving statistical capabilities, including the institution of a National Education Infrastructure Management System (NEIMS)
- school construction and infrastructure expenditure, including the reduction of personnel costs as a percentage of total expenditure
- the Foundations for Learning Campaign to encourage the basics of reading and numeracy through strong foundational skills

- the recommendation to put in place a National Education Evaluation Development Unit (NEEDU) that may provide the basis for external and expert oversight and supervision of teachers
- the Quality Learning and Teaching Campaign to unify education stakeholders, including teachers and officials, and to hold them to minimum standards of behaviour expected for delivering quality education.

Nonetheless, unfortunately this range of praiseworthy programmes do not seem to be energising the school system in a new direction and in the intended ways. Chapter 3 told the story of failures in education today. Maybe it is too soon to tell, but it seems apparent that there is not really traction on the ground or a combination of the solutions into a dynamic package that has its own forward momentum.

Elephants in the room

There are two further obvious issues that are being ignored. They need much more careful consideration, and will just be noted here.

The first is the question of the ex-model-C schools, now morphed into section 21 schools, a model that effectively allows schools to raise and manage their own funds in addition to the departmental subsidy. The ability to charge higher school fees in the suburbs was a rational decision to add to the resources available in the school system and to allow the shifting of state resources to the poorer schools. It has meant a jewel of excellence in the school system, one more highly funded and able to ensure significantly higher pupil achievement levels.

This undoubtedly takes on a racial dimension in that the bulk of the children in the schools continue to be largely white suburban residents. Generally the schools are economically in the top 20%, though in many instances the demographics of student intake have shifted dramatically. Anecdotal evidence tells of taxis pouring out of townships in the morning in an attempt by township children to ensure access to better quality suburban education. However, the teaching staff has in most cases stayed predominantly white, with questions thus being asked about cultural sensitivity and role modelling.

The legal requirement for a process of fee exemptions for poorer children has also put many of these schools under pressure. Inequalities have sometimes been a target of demands around schooling, with the ex-model-C schools a soft target in such calls. The bottom line is that the dynamic in these schools is little understood and subject to much prejudice and assumption. More importantly, the discussion has been deeply unsatisfactory in relation to their place, role and contribution in the overall improvement of quality education. I pick up on this in Chapter 5.

At this point, let it simply be said that the place of these schools is not in itself going to determine the extent of improvements in township and rural education. In a direct sense, the suburban schools are too few to absorb all those in poor schools, and they would be a diversion and misdirection of attention from the more difficult but pressing task of improving poor schools. Chasing the parents into private education would not free up resources. Nonetheless, they are a part of the overall system whose needs should be sensitively addressed to serve the overall national needs more effectively.

The second issue is the question of language. Evidence seems to show that it helps to learn the foundations of conceptual development – to learn basic literacy and numeracy – in your home language, whether this is Zulu, Pedi, Japanese or Arabic. A switch to English as a common language then becomes easier after about four to five years of mother-tongue education.

Obviously, questions around home language could be complex in a multilanguage, multiethnic environment. Apart from English, Afrikaans has been the most successful example of development of mother-tongue language materials and teaching in South African schooling. Yet Afrikaans was clearly tied to a complex struggle for language, cultural, economic and nationalist rights and to a movement that sought state power and resources.

Today, the mobilisation for other-tongue social movements is low, parents are divided and conflicted on the issue, and the availability of a range of materials is even more limited. While the constitution emphasises the right of all to be addressed by the state in the language of their choice, the reality of materials availability severely limits this right at present. Mother-tongue educators in indigenous languages are few and far between.

This will have to be faced. If there is to be serious redress around language, vast funds and resources will have to be made available. The debate has not really gone beyond rhetorical flourishes and gestures to the rights-based demands of language education. How much of a priority is the country prepared to make it? I do not have an answer.

5 | Schools getting it right

Piet N Aphane High School, under the leadership of headmaster Nare Annanias Moloto, is situated in Magatle Village, near Lebowakgomo in rural Limpopo. In 2009 it celebrated its twelfth anniversary. Its slogan, 'Hard work pays dividends', is reflected above all in two things.

Firstly, its matric pass rate has improved from a dismal 18% in 1998 to 91% in 2003 (dropping to 85% and then some 80% in recent years). Secondly, through creative fundraising, the school has a science and biology lab, a media centre soon-to-be and home economics centre 'which is today known as the Technology Centre and Permakitchen'. A range of academic streams and active sports clubs complement a programme of visits that has taken learners as far afield as Robben Island, Cape Point, the Pretoria Police Museum and KwaZulu-Natal sugar fields, where they 'learnt a lot about science and biology'.[97] Students enter Olympiads and at least six learners are on school tertiary bursaries.

Yet the object of the school's biggest pride is its vegetable gardens and sites for permaculture and agroforestry. Not only does the school supply and train surrounding schools, but the post office, police, clinics and others have benefited too. Boreholes, rain-harvesting and a whole environmental policy have enthused and mobilised the village. Parents also use the school buildings on Wednesday evenings for services and functions for the dominant Zionist church in the village, thus seeing the school as a community resource.

In the school's words, taken from its application to an awards trust:

(We congratulate you) for wanting to know more about what is happening in schools. Piet N Aphane never said that 'Manna will come from Heaven'. Piet N Aphane had to be an early bird that caught the fattest worm since 1994. And we don't have a community or SGB [school governing body] serving like an opposition party. However, we achieve all these through team-work, hard work, as the motto of our school says, through sacrificing our time, e.g. coming to work even during the holidays and weekends; and over and above all conveying our efforts to the Celestial Surgeon [God].[98]

I wrote an article for the Helen Suzman Foundation[99] that quoted Piet N Aphane's achievements. Whether for reasons of good journalism or because they doubted my claims, they sent a photographer to visit the school. There are proud photographs that now accompany the article, of parents – ordinary rural mamas – farming the productive school vegetable gardens, and of the sign at the school entrance. The 'Environmental Policy' is posted above the School Policy in neat letters, urging the students to 'respect our trees, flowers and vegetables', not to litter in the school grounds, to use water and electricity sparingly and to 'reuse, repair and recycle'.

The School Policy too is worth noting. It emphasises that the school 'is a drug- and weapon-free zone', and that everyone must 'respect our school property' and 'promote community involvement in our projects'.

It seems churlish in the face of what has been achieved here to remind ourselves that education in our country is in crisis and our youth have an uncertain future. Rather, what we can say is that it is possible to do something about it. In one remote village, deciding to make a difference himself, Principal Moloto has shown that there is a way.

He phones me every two months or so, a regular call to keep me informed and updated about what is happening in his school. He phones to explain and discuss what has happened with exam results, such as the matrics, or other matters. He is often actively fundraising and pressuring corporate givers and education trusts to back his schemes – from equipment, buildings and labs to field trips for his learners – though he does not ask for anything from me. Rather, he understands the importance of networks and of regular communication. We have become friends and often share education experiences.

Incidentally, Moloto's son and daughter have gone into engineering and technology fields at Gauteng universities of technology, scarce skills the country desperately requires. Yet these polite, hard-working youngsters have been thrown in at the deep end by their universities, with little support or appropriate assistance. Somehow too they have had to find firms willing to take them on for practical experience, without which they could not academically advance. All they lack are the networks to advance their skills or the supports to provide clear direction and assistance in their search, but something seems to be breaking down in the higher education institutions, which abdicate any responsibility. It is not surprising they struggle to get graduates through their systems.

Piet N Aphane is not the only school, nor Moloto the only principal doing it right. There are many examples throughout the country. Let me quote from another document by Dr Mduduzi Mathe, the headmaster of Bhukulani High School in Soweto, delivered at a workshop on why schools work, held at the Development Bank of Southern Africa in March 2009. Bhukulani was a school visited by President Jacob Zuma, who praised the state of education at the school, explained his own situation as someone who had had to leave school early in primary school, and encouraged the pupils to learn hard. Mathe's lessons for the solid achievements of his school, including a matric pass rate of more than 90%, are clear: schools work, and have over thousands of years worked, simply because there are people who are prepared to work. A school becomes a school, a working school for that matter, because:

> . . . there is a head of the institution who is a credible leader, not lazy, 'always' there and, most importantly, a visionary; there is a

working School Management Team (SMT) which shares and works for one common goal – that is, to promote and work (incessantly) for, and towards the school's vision (dream) . . . ; there are educators who go to class on time . . . and, most importantly, focus on teaching when in class rather than on things that will not help the child to move on to the next grade the following year; the School Governing Body [provides] the necessary support and [governs] the school rather than opting to take over the day-to-day activities of the school, which are the responsibility of the principal and the SMT.

Mathe also emphasised that teachers should attend cluster meetings, workshops and other training for educators so that the teachers can meet all the assessment requirements. Lastly, he said that learners must be receptive and willing to be educated.

> This is, in my candid opinion, a given once the school is reputed and perennially working for meaningful education and ultimately, encouraging results. By encouraging results I mean ensuring that out of every ten learners, nine pull through. An ideal situation is to ensure that all learners pass at the end of the year!
>
> In conclusion, I would like to point out that it is possible to mould and change the attitudes of learners. It is not easy but, I emphasise, is achievable. A positive mind yields positive results . . . At Bhukulani [these] things are happening and, therefore, encouraging results are achieved. The role of the leader cannot be overemphasised! [100]

At the same workshop Gladys Ramasela Selepe, principal of Sakhile Primary School in Ratanda, gave input. Ratanda is a little township in the poverty-stricken Vaal area. The school was started in 1972 and goes up to Grade 8. I was struck by the quiet leadership Selepe had showed in a Wits executive management course for principals, and her obvious ability to draw together the staff in her school to achieve key aims.

The strongest impression I had of her was of her description of walking up and down the corridors to be fully in tune with what is happening in her school, where teachers and learners are, to make sure she has a hands-on and sympathetic touch when it comes to dealing with daily problems.

Many of her approaches echo those of Dr Mathe. There is a detailed set of planning processes and systems to ensure success, no magic formulae. It is her combination of strategic vision with detailed knowledge of the workings of her school that is the source of her strength and determination. Her comments are worth quoting at length, for the practical and detailed insight they give into how school leadership can make a difference if it is focused and clear.

> Find something that you truly desire and love and live for it like this is your last chance. Find a strength inside to tackle life in every aspect of it, you shall be rewarded in the process. That is what educators at Sakhile Primary School believe in, they have truly found that thing which is to teach and nurture learners to be the best amongst the best . . .
>
> The school does its planning for the following year in October of the current year. All educators first hold a meeting to choose themes, thereafter they break into phases where they develop work schedules and work programmes under the supervision of an HOD for that phase. Finally they break into learning areas. Here educators do team planning . . .
>
> [As far as organisation goes, the] Deputy Principal, who is in charge of curriculum, organises departments according to different learning areas and the Deputy Principal in charge of administration divides the administration work between the two administrators. Finally, the Deputy Principal makes sure that all the systems in the office or in the administration are good and ready to use.
>
> Management first meet as an SMT (Strategic Management Team), whereby the Principal tables agenda items and they are discussed

and decisions taken. Thereafter a staff meeting is convened where curriculum matters and circulars are communicated and interpreted to educators to forge common understanding within the institution, so that implementation becomes easy. All systems used within the school become transparent to minimise conflict. HODs control the curriculum offered by educators by doing class visits and making sure that they assess the work planned versus the work given to learners. After evaluation they compile reports and submit them once per month to the Deputy Principal in charge of curriculum. The Deputy then consolidates the report and presents it to the Principal. Learners are assessed on a quarterly basis and feedback is communicated to parents. Analysis of results is first discussed by the SMT and later taken to the entire staff, so that together we are able to improve teaching and learning. The consolidated report is then presented to the SGB and finally sent to the district office for their comment and further development.[101]

Pam Christie led a ministerial committee that examined successful schools.[102] A South African who now teaches in Australia, she has been writing for many years on ways to improve SA education, and helped to shape the Wits executive management course for principals (discussed later in this chapter). Her conclusion was that the principal of a school made a significant difference. Teachers needed the administrative efficiency and ordered predictability of a well-run school. They also needed pedagogical leadership, a space to reflect on how they were teaching and to continually re-establish goals and reinforce teaching strategies. Both of these required leadership from the principal.

Not that the principal had to do all these things, but he or she would need to be able to order and delegate, draw in teams and get people working themselves on presenting solutions. A principal was required to order and enthuse teaching strategies. In fact, the central purpose of the school was always seen to be to build a culture of teaching and learning, and to achieve relevant and appropriate educational outcomes. The whole purpose of the school should be to achieve results in the classroom. From this could flow the hiring of good teachers, working with parents or surrounding communities, and drawing in wider support including funding.

In the words of the ministerial committee, four dynamics stood out in strategies of schools that work. Firstly, all of the schools were focused on their central tasks of teaching, learning and management with a sense of purpose, responsibility and commitment. Secondly, they had strong organisational capacity, including leadership (in various forms) and management; and professionalism was valued. Thirdly, all of the schools carried out their tasks with competence and confidence; all had organisational cultures or mind-sets that supported hard work, expected achievement, and acknowledged success. And lastly, all had strong internal accountability systems in place, which enabled them to meet the demands of external accountability, particularly in terms of Senior Certificate achievement.[103]

All the schools celebrated achievement and found ways to acknowledge and reward high achievement among staff and students. All expected that the goals were to develop talents across a range of fields, including academic, sports, culture, music, service, and so on.

'Back to school' for principals

Linda Vilakazi-Tselane is confident and articulate, focused but warm. She is coordinator of the Wits executive management course for principals and senior teachers. The course is run at the Wits School of Education, which is headed by Mary Metcalfe, a former MEC for education in Gauteng.

On a Saturday morning once a month, hundreds of principals and school departmental heads meet to upgrade their understanding of their context and their work. There are ten sessions. They usually consist of an expert input or even a motivational speech, touching on education and its importance, but also looking at failings in the education system, the history of black education and issues in management. Then the educators form groups of some fifteen to twenty, to reflect on the inputs and their conceptual assumptions. District officers are also part of this programme, which is arranged to group together principals in a district so that they can share experiences and ideas. Afterwards, principals have a more task-oriented lecture and often spend the afternoon learning 'hard' skills such as computer use or timetabling using particular software.

They have tasks on a monthly basis, both writing up summaries of the material delivered and often engaging with other teachers or stakeholders in the school environment. A lot of effort is geared to drawing up and interacting with the school's SIP, or School Improvement Plan, a compulsory part of the school calendar that is often treated in a very mechanical and bureaucratic way. In 2008, the first year this course was held, there were some 200 principals; by the second year, it was bursting at the seams with over 400 participants.

There is no formal accredited qualification at the end, merely a certificate of recognition from Wits for this special achievement. Yet senior teachers and principals were there regularly on Saturday mornings when they could have been shopping or simply sleeping in. I learned an enormous amount about the detail of the issues that they face, the difficulties of the communities in which they are situated, and their enormous desire to improve themselves and do well by their young charges.

I have two outstanding memories. One was when a principal from Selborne Primary in Vereeniging came to give her end-of-year presentation. Selborne was created in a tent in a concentration camp for the children of prisoners during the Boer War. Now it is serving a new disadvantaged community. Like the school to which it is a feeder, Generaal Smuts Hoërskool, it has totally transformed its demographics with much the same dedicated staff still in place. When I asked the principal about the Wits course, she explained that she had previously hit a wall in her career and did not know how to climb it. Then she burst into tears as she tried to explain all that the course had done for her. It gave her a safe space to explore what were generic problems of the system and what, within these, were issues she could deal with. It made her see the reasons why she had arrived at a place that seemed to offer no way out, and enabled her to grapple with the achievable differences she might be able to make. She said that the course made her feel empowered to rebuild a team around her that would be able to tackle some of these challenges.

My other memory was standing on the stage in my academic gown during the graduation ceremony while the graduates in the auditorium literally held up their certificates for us to see, dancing and singing to praise us as the coordinators or facilitators, proud and resolute in what they had achieved.

How did they do it? What were the successful ingredients of the course? There was a careful curriculum, partly designed by Pam Christie, which took teachers methodically through the key issues in education. They realised that failings were systemic and not simply due to peculiarities of their own school or context. They were forced into solutions mode, not being allowed to wallow in problems and criticisms. They had to identify intervention points and work out how to respond at their own school level, in interaction with other staff who would have to be their allies. In short, a comfortable space was created in which they could reflect and move forward in a guided way.

Linda Vilakazi-Tselane is assured about what ultimately created this space. The principals were treated with dignity. The course was a real one, which tested them. They were given readings and books, which were theirs to use and study. Outputs were expected from them. In return, they were treated like the experienced and essential educators they are. Attention was given to making sure they had a proper breakfast and lunch, to making sure the seminar rooms were decent and the input speakers were people worth listening to.

It is also extremely praiseworthy that the entire course was financed generously by the Gauteng Department of Education, in full, without skimping and cutting costs unnecessarily. This willingness to back an innovative attempt to address senior educators in this way was very bold and deserves to be commended.

So what is the moral of this story? It appears that if you prepare carefully, if you are willing to take the detailed trouble and to pay the costs that such attention requires, if you are willing to listen but also to guide and demand performance, then new ground can be broken. We will have to see what impact this particular course has on the lives of the principals and the outcomes in Gauteng.

There are many other courses to support principals and teachers. Some are good and some are mediocre or bad. But this one shows that there are models that can work. The schools of education, and other providers and trainers, should put their heads together and see how similar processes can be started elsewhere and with new groups of principals. Principals are key stakeholders in the schools, central to organisation and inspiration. The energy required to listen to them and help set them on a road of progress is surely worth every bit of attention it requires.

How can model-C schools contribute?

The former model-C schools grew out of an arrangement in the first transition to democracy, where formerly white schools were encouraged to be part of the public school system but were able to raise funds from parents as an extra contribution to education quality. Latterly, they have had section 21 status conferred on them, a choice many schools have made because of the rights to raise and spend discretionary funds.

These schools, perhaps better called 'suburban' schools, perform well. They are generally organised, focused and able to draw on experienced teachers. Due to their access to middle-class constituencies, they can afford additional resources. As previous beneficiaries of the white education system, their facilities and physical infrastructure are on the whole significantly better than those of the township schools, and might include such things as adequate staff rooms, a computer laboratory, a functioning library, even sports fields and a swimming pool. But their ability to raise and utilise extra funding from their middle-class parent base provides visible proof of the inequalities that remain in education.

They have inherited a particular history of benefiting from apartheid and the privileges of white society, leaving them open to criticism of being elitist. Their excellence does at face value perpetuate inequalities in that so many other schools do badly. But the solution is clearly to focus on improving the schools where the majority of learners are. The suburban schools could never admit big enough numbers of black students for access itself to become the solution. Even if all white students were chased out, at maximum these schools would represent 10% of the spaces available in public schools. Bad schooling would still exist in most of the township and rural schools.

Although many suburban schools have already admitted large numbers of black learners, the question remains whether they have opened up enough. I have seen an Afrikaans school on the East Rand where all the *joggies*, or high performers, were white. The children were performing and being acknowledged in a fabulous range of activities and spheres. But I wondered aloud whether they were being done a service by being kept from a black populace; whether they would be building the networks that might stand them in good business and political stead later in life.

Then, on the other hand, there are schools like Generaal Smuts Hoërskool in Vereeniging, a formerly Afrikaans school that shows the extent to which a model-C, suburban school can change. It is being managed with love and extreme care by principal Ronald Bartie. He loves his children and beams with pride at the high achievers and what they are able to accomplish, the opportunities the school creates for the children, from debating, drama and music to academic, sporting and Olympiad competitions. Almost 97% of the children are black Africans from the townships and suburbs around the Vaal.

The picture of the staff in the school's 2008 yearbook shows a dedicated group of ordinary classroom teachers with years of service, and predominantly Afrikaans. The yearbook begins with a quote from the preamble to South Africa's constitution, 'To improve the life of all citizens and free the potential of each person.' As Bartie argues:

Notwithstanding somewhat difficult economic circumstances, we have managed to not only lead and encourage young lives in their search for knowledge, but support many of those who have to face the hardship of loss and deprivation. The gifted and dedicated staff have gone the extra mile to assist parents in building the characters of their children. It provides much pleasure to the staff; it is in fact a calling.[104]

Bartie goes on to say that the school's educators work from 7 a.m. to 10 p.m. on most days, with cluster meetings, portfolio meetings, training sessions, extra-mural activities and marking.

With the number of meetings that needs to be attended (all educational) and the amount of preparation and marking that needs to be done, an educator has very little time for his/her family life. But there is no other occupation that is so gratifying. When learners realise that they are 'in charge' of their futures . . . and all of a sudden they begin to work . . . they seem to change overnight and become responsible young adults, who strive for perfection. The educator is rewarded with the knowledge that he/she had an impact on their lives.[105]

I can attest that these words are more than rhetoric; Generaal Smuts school is performing an act of citizenship, of transformation and of unselfish patriotism without equal that deserves to be emulated. Most of the suburban schools want to do well by the children they serve, want to ensure that all the children of South Africa have access to their high standards of achievement.

In many instances, from a third to 40% of learners at suburban schools are black Africans. They are often the children of domestics or workers in the area, or they taxi in from the nearest or even quite distant townships, where their parents might be teachers, civil servants, shop workers, lower middle-class or well-paid workers desperate to ensure some education opportunities for their children. For many township children, however, the fees of say R15 000 to R20 000 per annum are totally unaffordable. Departmental formulae insist on a fee exemption process, but do not cap this or subsidise it.

There is enormous pressure on the suburban schools to open up, as perhaps there should be. At the same time, reports are that many of the schools are creaking and that the funding model of a form of internal cross-subsidisation is not sustainable. In many cases, the schools find themselves financially squeezed and struggle to balance their books and maintain the range of courses and activities that they would prefer. But government can hardly be expected to spend even more on the richer children than on poor children.

Policy in the early days of democracy decided to allow a bifurcated system in the interests of tapping additional voluntary resources and funds, and in the interests of preserving a particular tradition of excellence. It is no use targeting these schools or treating them as elitist islands. Rather, how can they be harnessed as a national resource that can contribute to the overall improvement as we strive for quality education for all? What is the solution to ensure the maintenance of the order and achievement of the suburban schools while increasing access?

Another question is, how do these schools contribute in a stronger fashion to the demands of transformation? For instance, their teaching staff remains predominantly white. Can this easily be changed when the majority of teaching students at universities are still white females?

Few black students want to enter teaching, underpaid and under-resourced as it is. One can only speculate as to the reasons. It is hard to say whether the opening up of career opportunities for blacks has moved teaching down the ladder of desirability for them. We also need to understand why so many of the teacher trainees are young white girls, clearly dedicated to the idea of teaching and willing to put up with lowish salaries.

What should the suburban schools do – poach the best teachers from township schools?

There needs to be discussion about which problems we want to address. How can their internal transformation realistically be managed and what are realistic targets? How do they extend their support and outreach into the wider system?

Anthea Cereseto is principal at Parktown Girls High in Johannesburg, a wonderful racially mixed public school. She is active in her union, NAPTOSA, and chairperson of the SA Council for Educators (SACE). She argues that as an older generation, we often impose our prejudices and stereotypes on youngsters. For example, we are obsessed with race because of the past from which we have emerged. Many of the younger children do not understand the problem. Learning and mixing happen spontaneously. Yes, there are levels at which white and black pupils might group together or separate, but there are myriad activities in the classroom and extra-murally where they share, talk, learn from each other.[106]

It is often a top-down, old-fashioned imposition that wants a conscious attempt to address diversity, for example. Yet addressing racism and sexism during the course of a language class might be a better place than in a series of departmental workshops. Difference and diversity are obviously two of the values that need to be tackled. The approach to the suburban schools should not entrench old racial habits but help with their solution.

Cereseto also argues that the best form of outreach and sharing is probably through building professional communities of interest. She does not yet see much evidence of working consistently to address quality across schools, though the structure of districts does encourage contact across the divides. The basis has to be laid, though. In Parktown's case, it has twinned with two Soweto schools, and teachers might often swop schools to experience different approaches and systems.[107]

There is an enormous range of schools that fall into the category of 'former model-C'. Those that are deliberately trying to hold back transformation, which might use language or their autonomous rights to keep change out, are probably an extreme few. Some have tried to retain their language character or the demographics of white dominance, or to keep out too many non-fee-paying pupils from surrounding townships. In some, there have been incidents of racism, of violence between pupils, of assaults on teachers, and suggestions of bullying and unfair initiation practices.

Yet others, like Ronald Bartie's in Vereeniging, have completely changed the demographics of attendance at their schools. Generaal Smuts Hoërskool continues to maintain the same teaching and school achievements, though Bartie's staff is predominantly white and his pupils black. Most suburban schools have a substantial black presence, and many have embraced change and their place in the new South Africa with enthusiasm and initiative. We need to see them as part of the public system and try to understand how they can contribute in raising the bar in this system. It is by accepting their bona fides and playing to their strengths, rather than treating these once-white suburban schools as soft targets, that we may make progress and enhance their contribution.

The suburban schools should be seen as a resource to the system as a whole. It is a generally well-functioning part of the overall system that should be preserved and encouraged. A new education authority with a renewed education strategy should look for ways to be sympathetic towards the difficulties and needs of the suburban schools. This will not happen automatically; I think these schools should do more to engage publicly, to position themselves, to debate the issues openly, and to show the ways in which they can contribute to the overall welfare of the children of South Africa.

In the first place, these schools are themselves centres of excellence. They enable large numbers of the next generation, whether black or white, to engage the benefits of knowledge and learning. Their outcomes indicate that they get the basics of education and learning right.

The reasons for this are worth understanding because there are lessons that can be learned and applied elsewhere. Undoubtedly, superior resources – financial, physical, human – can be called upon in the predominantly middle-class communities. On the whole, there is better management and planning than in the majority of schools.

Curricula and their delivery are more strictly ordered, and teachers are clear in their aims and are subject to scrutiny and monitoring. The school day is not left to chance, and is ordered and predictable – qualities often lacking in township schools. Teachers generally have a sounder subject knowledge and spend more hours working, including extra-mural activities, than in township schools.

Clearly, these experiences and many of the tools and techniques could be shared with township schools. Much of this could be done in direct exchange between teachers – as in the case of Parktown Girls and the Soweto schools – and in sharing their daily practice and curriculum tasks. Facilities at schools can also be made available, such as sports fields or swimming pools for galas and lessons.

In the first place, teachers should teach their students to think and to love learning. Then, too, the pupils at the suburban schools need to be educated to be good citizens. Outreach and social concern and involvement would in any case be a useful part of any extra-mural activities. Perhaps the older generation is more obsessed by the dynamics of race and exclusion than the new more non-racial generation, but there are explicit things that can be done to intensify understanding and cultural exchange. Suburban pupils can visit the townships in ways that make them feel safe and are educational, as well as simply to get in direct contact with friends. Joint programmes focusing on cultural difference, identity and meaning can be arranged, as well as joint activities such as summer learning camps or wilderness experiences, where genuine friendships may develop across colour and class divisions. Only a sensitive teacher, empowered by innovative policies and school support, will know what is artificial and what has genuine educational and long-term benefits.

It is not just children who need to learn to cross boundaries. Parents, too, would benefit from the school being able to involve them in some of these activities. Certainly, teachers cannot in the end teach adequately without understanding the circumstances in which all their children live. The obvious need is for a workable strategy to change the demographics of teacher profiles – currently overwhelmingly white – at the suburban schools. It is possible to experiment and innovate without disrupting or damaging many of the positive patterns or trends at these schools. There are issues such as multilingualism or integration or dealing with social disadvantage that need unique solutions. Beyond this, teachers should be encouraged to get out of their natural comfort zones and take the trouble to explore the variety and diversity of the lives of different communities in South Africa. This can only benefit their teaching and their ability to support and educate their wards – from whichever community they come.

No one suggests such an agenda is easy. It needs careful thinking, and all the pros and cons should be explored. Nonetheless, we cannot sustain a pattern of largely white schools, of some schools continuing to benefit from historical privilege, and of the effective existence of two school systems in one country. The former white schools provide an important testing ground for new ideas in the battle for transformation. They are sites of excellent practice where many of the goals of the South African nation can be realised, if the schools are treated with sensitivity and care.

6 | A map for the future

Concern about the public school system and its shortcomings is widely and publicly expressed, and openly acknowledged by education authorities. These concerns found expression, among other places, within education resolutions at the ANC conference in Polokwane in December 2007. This important conference defined a far more grassroots-based approach by the ruling party that was geared to popular mobilisation (and of course saw the election of Jacob Zuma as ANC president).

In education, there was a call for attention to the impacts of poverty on schooling. Two specific areas include nutrition schemes and the increasing of non-fee-paying schools to 60% of schools (from 40%). Crucially, there was a call to 'restore teaching to the noble profession' it had once been. In return for this commitment by society, teachers were to reciprocate by being 'in class, on time, teaching'.[108] It was argued that education must go beyond being a concern of the education department to become the concern of government as a whole. The ANC subcommittee on education was charged to give flesh to such formulations, as well as to develop a plan that could inform its election platform dynamics in the field of education.

Most policy choice sounds terribly conscious in retrospect but is often a series of actions adding up to 'muddling through'. By June 2008, a combination of external concern with the state of education and the internal positioning of the Development Bank of Southern Africa (DBSA) prompted DBSA Board chair Jay Naidoo to take action. Through networks and connections, this previous cabinet minister and well-respected social activist brought together three key people to suggest the drawing up of an Education Roadmap. They were the education minister, Naledi Pandor; the head of the ANC education subcommittee, Zweli Mkhize, who would have a strong influence on appointments and direction of the incoming government (in fact, strictly speaking, head of the ANC Social Transformation Committee); and the DBSA chair himself. The DBSA's successful positioning in the education policy space over the years enabled it to be seen as a critical and honest broker in the stakeholder policy process.

I need to declare an interest. As an education specialist employed by the DBSA I was involved in implementing the Education Roadmap process. I found it exciting and believe it has come up with an excellent set of priorities and key interventions.

In 2007 I argued at a conference[109] that education change is enormously complex and outcomes often seem impervious to policy intervention. I added that we needed to put forward a comprehensive coordinated approach to education policy, to develop planning, targets and priorities for the medium term, and to elaborate a clear national consensus among stakeholders. I called for a strong and principle-driven commitment to increased involvement in the education arena. This would also have to explore the range of non-school interventions that need to be coordinated and drawn together to have an impact on schooling. It was to tackle just these issues that the Education Roadmap process was implemented.

Plotting the way ahead

On the initiative of the three principal partners, Naidoo, Pandor and Mkhize, the DBSA agreed to convene a stakeholder process to examine problems in schooling and develop possible solutions. The participants represented a range of ANC-aligned and non-ANC-aligned institutions, unions, government officials, academics, NGOs and other commentators. While not a representative forum as such, these would either represent key education stakeholders or carry the respect of stakeholders in the field.

The process began in July 2008 with an analysis of key problem areas. This followed the Carnoy framework discussed in Chapter 4 –

the in-school level, how to give schools the support they need, and the societal factors that affect the readiness of students to learn. A set of suggested priorities for intervention was put forward and fashioned into a ten-point programme that was released for public discussion. *Business Day* spontaneously ran the document on its website.

The Roadmap highlighted five key areas that hold back education. First, it showed how social disadvantage is reproduced across generations, where parents are often uneducated, relatively powerless and lack information. Second, teachers were seen as key to education improvement. A range of issues affect teachers, from poor subject knowledge and teaching practices, to insufficient numbers in training and little performance evaluation. Third, it focused on dysfunctional schools, accepting that schools mostly do not achieve acceptable outcomes, reinforced by confusion over OBE. Schools are badly managed and supported. The departmental Foundations for Learning Campaign was noted for beginning to address issues of reading and numeracy at primary and foundation level, where it counts most.

Fourth was the question of resources. Despite massive improvements, there are still huge backlogs: lack of libraries, labs and computers, not to mention poverty effects, from nutrition and AIDS orphans to gang violence. And finally, on the question of responsibility and accountability, it was acknowledged that far stronger national intervention is needed to overcome inefficiencies as policy drops down to provincial delivery levels. District support systems and management in particular need to be fixed to give impetus to school-level improvement.

It was envisaged that the government would consider these findings and recommendations. Beyond this, the process provided the basis for a debate on education and education priority interventions. It opened up discussion of the need for a social compact of key stakeholders that could, through common purpose and collective action, achieve a more effective education system and better education outcomes.

In 2009 South Africa had an exciting election and chose the ANC with a landslide victory. The new government will want to treat the process as one of many inputs in a complex web of policy-making processes. New education ministers and a new cabinet, as well as provincial ministers and top officials, were appointed. Over time, policy direction will become solidified and clearer. More importantly, we will see the concrete and practical plans that are meant to determine future direction.

Starting a national debate

The Education Roadmap was a process that presents a number of ways of doing things that could be fruitful. It has come up with a plan for discussion. At last, there is a set of recommended priorities that could become the basis for a focused discussion, and I would be surprised if many of its focus areas are changed dramatically. They may play a significant role in the planning of the new government and new education administration.

But of course the Roadmap has limitations. It may be that many of its lessons are specific and unrepeatable; it is more likely that a series of lessons and comparisons may be drawn for more effective strategic alignment and policy development in a range of differing situations. There may well be things left out, but a discussion would allow these to be identified. The crux is not that the ten points drawn up are the final word or even necessarily the best ten points. Rather, the Roadmap says let us have a common discussion and develop an agenda.

This should not be around too many issues. The brutal truth is that a number of actions together will be needed, that education is a complex field, but also that not everything can be changed at once. What are the crucial interventions that need to be made to overcome the main roadblocks? The number of these drivers will have to be limited. Over time, other things can be included, and no doubt the edges of work will always be fuzzy and allow for individualised efforts. But what the Education Roadmap does is to help focus and limit the number of issues that are up for intervention. It helps get a debate going on what the interventions should be and recommends a programme that could provide the basis for the final plan that needs to be drawn up.

The Roadmap is not that plan, but in my opinion it is a very good beginning. Its recommendations are made on the basis of a careful analysis of the available facts and on a realistic assessment of the nature and scale of problems.

The other aspect of the Roadmap that holds out lessons for policy development is its involvement of the key stakeholders. Not everyone is there. It does not claim to be a representative sample. But there is enough spread and ideological difference, enough specialist input and enough generic involvement to ensure that the process is wide and inclusive.

In particular, it includes the two main stakeholders – government and the teacher unions. There are enough others with clout, including the minister of education herself and the ANC, to hold both parties to account and insist they deal with the questions in an open way. There is also enough space in the way all the stakeholders are called on to cooperate, a rolling and extensive analysis and intense discussion, for everyone to feel they have had a chance to be heard and to put their concerns on the table.

The Roadmap is only a beginning. It shows the kind of process that is required, the involvement of expertise and of stakeholders on the ground, the involvement of officials and institutions with real clout, and the broad and inclusive agenda that enables wide public discussion and broad consensus to develop.

The ten-point programme has already stimulated debate. Former Gauteng MEC for education and Wits education head, Mary Metcalfe, thinks it right to focus on teachers, but feels outcomes-based performance pay is too complicated to work. (Though the point is still: what kind of accountability system will work?) The Roadmap argues for regular testing to keep parents informed, but some say teachers will be diverted by such exams and not focus on learning. The National Professional Teachers' Organisation of SA (NAPTOSA) has commented on how serious the ANC seems about education and seems to express hope for the implementation of the Polokwane emphasis on education as a social factor. Educationist Jonathan Jansen has called for ruthless pruning of institutions and officials where work is not happening. HSRC researcher Linda Chisholm has warned against rewriting curricula without also looking at the implications of a destabilised system and the requirements to support systems change. Nick Taylor of JET Education Services has suggested that ten points are too many. SADTU has called for the reopening of teachers' colleges and for renewed thrusts around teacher development.

A teachers' development summit is scheduled for 2009 that will involve all the teachers' organisations. A summit will not automatically solve all challenges and problems but it does propose an agenda of discussion and it does provide a common space for commitments and promises of initiative. There is a critical debate emerging around the role of teacher unions, specifically SADTU, spurred by some of the more outrageous statements coming from within regional leadership.

All of this is as it should be. For the Roadmap proposals are not just a set of technical points. Profoundly social processes like education need debate and social consensus, with complexity as well as focused impact. Points need to be debated individually, but also as part of an overall package because it is also how the totality of challenges are addressed that will make the difference.

As I have shown, there was a careful and slow, ultimately democratic engagement with various stakeholders, quite meticulous in the space it gave to be heard and to discuss. The education department may have acknowledged that programmes are not working or finding traction in the way they ought, that systems change is much more complex than they could have imagined. Teachers' unions have been able to own some (grudging) responsibility. A framework of priorities guides citizens seeking ways to intervene, which will be discussed in more detail in Chapter 7 – alumni returning to schools to build networks of access for poor children, corporates searching for effective corporate social investment, graduates willing to do national service in the front line of schools. The dialogue has already seen shifts in attitudes and acknowledgment of the enormous tasks ahead. More deep discussion is needed, and perhaps ultimately a social pact that binds teachers, their unions, departmental officials, political leadership and parents, as well as learners themselves.

Important contributors to South Africa's poor education outcomes arise from institutional weaknesses within the public education system, problems in 'delivery' by education departments and officials, and the range of problems faced by teachers in ensuring effective teacher development. There is a need for an approach that will improve the efficiency and accountability of the system at the same time as improving support to and accountability of the teaching corps.

What should not be underestimated is the extent to which the Roadmap process – and a wider, more comprehensive stakeholder engagement process – may contribute to national debate and help focus discussion around core elements that may lead to solutions. The impact is clearly difficult to measure, though the level of media interest may indicate public awareness and focus. It remains to be seen whether the concurrence of situation and circumstance, and the underlying assumptions of the model of policy development, intervention and change, make enough sense to see positive policy transformation and implementation in the future.

Furthermore, there is the point about how citizens get their social institutions to participate in education. Granted, this is easier in a development bank with a key worry about skills, and granted it did not involve a stretch in relation to an accepted definition of 'social infrastructure' in the bank I work for, DBSA. Nonetheless, whether by corporates, NGOs, citizen initiatives, even reading groups, ways need to be found in all our structures and institutions to contribute to education improvement and to align our organisations to contribute.

The Education Roadmap, coordinated but not owned by DBSA, has offered one chance to put our education on track. It is not a holy grail; it is a space we need to understand and fill. It stimulates the sort of debate we need to focus on, the sort of approach the policy makers and politicians responsible for education in a new government will need to adopt.

We cannot fix everything at once. Many factors have an impact on education, many things go wrong. It is impossible to fix them all. There is a small window, post-Polokwane, post-democratic elections, to raise into public debate what we know about failures, to get agreement and to focus on priorities for the future. Money alone is not the issue, as South Africa has a relatively high education spend. What are the ten things we can really concentrate on, that will bring us the best and fastest results?

There are no guarantees: debate now will surely have an impact directly on the government and the new minister – in fact, ministers of education, including a new higher education portfolio. If the Roadmap succeeds, it will be by starting a grand national debate. What do we want from education, what are we going to do to get it right, what do we expect to achieve, by when?

The debate has hardly begun, after fifteen years of democratic space.

Ten-point programme of the Education Roadmap[110]

A. In-school

1. Teachers to be in class, on time, teaching. Teachers also to be required to use textbooks in class.
2. Focus efforts on improving the quality of early childhood education and primary schools, including implementing the Foundations for Learning Campaign emphasising the promotion of language and numeracy.
3. Conduct external tests for all Grade 3 and Grade 6 learners every year, and provide the results to parents.
4. Ensure effective evaluation of all teachers based on extent to which learner performances improve, with results influencing occupationally specific dispensation pay for teachers.
5. Enhance recruitment of quality teachers and strengthen teacher development:

- Offer bursaries to attract quality student intake into teacher training institutions and offer student loan repayments to attract young graduates into teacher contracts.
- Enhance pre-service and in-service teacher training, including through better coordination and resourcing.
- Ensure that teacher unions have a formal and funded role in teacher development.

B. Support to school

6. Strengthen management capacity to ensure working districts and schools. This entails bringing in management capacity from the private sector, civil society and elsewhere in the public sector.
   - Phase in a process of measurable improvements through targeting efforts at selected education districts and dysfunctional schools.
   - Use of infrastructure budgets as an incentive for schools that deliver improved teaching and learning.
7. Increase the use of Information and Communications Technology (ICT) in education, including audiovisual teaching materials in the classroom to supplement teaching and demonstrate quality teaching to learners and educators.
8. Improve national-provincial alignment and efficiency of education expenditure, through procuring textbooks nationally and allocating resources to improve district capacity. In this regard, the use of conditional grants is an important tool to ensure alignment.

C. Societal

9. Develop a social compact for quality education. This will include a National Consultative Forum dedicated to clarifying the 'non-negotiables' and performance targets for key stakeholders, and the monitoring thereof.
   - Mobilisation of communities at all levels should be encouraged to raise awareness and participation in education issues.

Examples include graduates assisting their former/dysfunctional schools, corporate social investment, party branch campaigns to clean up schools, supporting food gardens, and encouraging young graduates to enter teaching (Teach SA).

10. Implement poverty-combating measures that improve the environment for learning and teaching, such as a nutrition programme (cross-cutting programme with health), basic infrastructure for schools, and social support for children.

7 | The right mix

Positive change will require the combined efforts of all institutions and individuals interested in education. If we make a start now, if we have a plan so that efforts are broadly in line with an over-arching framework, it is possible that we will begin to see improve-ments within ten years or more. If work is comprehensive and multi-dimensional, and clearly led by a goal-directed education department, our efforts to improve quality can start to gain traction, and the syn-ergies will see long-term gains that cannot be reversed. No contribu-tion will be insignificant if it is part of this thrust to turn our schools around within a generation or two.

Corporate social investment (CSI) can make a huge difference. Over the years CSI has literally meant billions of Rand put into education, but the continuously poor outcomes in the system as a whole have resulted in a range of responses. In general, there is a sense of despair, and investors are desperate to know where to put their money. The old strategy of throwing money and resources at the problem clearly has not worked.

Somehow the schools themselves have been slow to take up the benefits of programmes and appear too internally shambolic to see improvements. Government has also not responded in efficient and supportive ways in many cases. Responses have resulted in much more careful attention being paid to research and trying to understand when things might work and why.

One example is the Zenex Foundation's analyses in the area of math-ematics and the attempts to design and fine-tune appropriate school support strategies – part of a ten-year CSI support programme an-nounced in 2005. As Zenex has implemented its strategies for maths improvement, it has hired researchers or scholars to ensure proper monitoring and evaluation along the way. Thus, it has been able to identify schools in which to work and to suggest why these schools seem to improve; it has been able to develop both teacher and student improvement plans; it has also been able to take teachers from public schools and place them in independent schools to be mentored.

Thus its solutions have not relied on wild claims or optimistic hope, but have pointed to the need for evidence-based policy development and implementation. This is as much a need for government as it is for private or corporate contributions to educational quality improvement. It also helps provide suggestions, models and policy lessons in attempts to expand on a greater scale. (One fascinating insight has been that maths improvement also requires literacy and reading improvement).

A more despairing approach has been to give up on government and adopt an anti-state approach to education. Clearly, this is not viable in an era where the rampant neoliberal approaches of unfettered markets are again open to question. A version of this has been to leave dysfunctional schools alone altogether, arguing that it is only in schools that are already functioning properly that results can be achieved. Sometimes this might mean selecting better-performing schools or better-performing teachers to be trained, or even better-performing students to receive special treatment, attention and perhaps bursaries.

This has not been completely out of line with government approaches. For instance, the main aim of the Dinaledi ('Star') schools has been to identify schools that already have a minimum rate of maths achievement, and to focus government expenditure and effort on these selected schools in order to improve maths and technology-oriented outputs. The Department of Education has also invited corporates to 'adopt' particular schools or clusters of Dinaledi schools and to input further resources, skills and attention to achieve the goal of maths passes. There is some evidence that the schools are already showing better results than other schools.[111]

As a strategy, however, it has the downside of being largely a strategy of despair. And it still does not answer the question of how to deal with those schools that will now get left even further behind. There is no automatic drag-up factor whereby better schools pull up their worse-performing siblings through the opposite of a trickle-down approach.

While there is nothing wrong with identifying a niche, while there is nothing wrong with assuming that even working-class children in dysfunctional schools deserve better opportunities, this cannot be elevated to the level of a principled approach. At best, there may be a niche for some of these 'elitist' possibilities, though one should be aware of their dangers and limitations.

What has become clear is that a scatter-gun approach will not work; rather, the approach needs to be much more like hand-holding. In this model, a corporate donor commits to working with particular schools, builds different components and commits to staying the course over a longer period. The relationship is more akin to a partnership than that of donor and recipient.

The advantage of something like a Roadmap (discussed in Chapter 6), or an agreed national set of priorities, is that it provides a framework of expectations and emphases within which corporates may choose areas of work where they have strengths, knowing that all sorts of stakeholders are on board to support these areas in different ways. In this model, government responses too would be much less arbitrary.

Without limiting the specific contribution that corporates can make – especially their specialist skills, the addition of resources to schools that are in need and show signs of meaningful initiative, and the ability to seed innovative ideas and programmes – such an approach helps ensure a greater alignment of the individual efforts of companies that want to make a difference, but may or may not themselves have appropriate expertise in education.

I have been involved with one such effort, which of course has not been going long enough to bear results. As a trustee of the Lafarge Education Trust, I have found myself working in a small rural village in the North West. All the problems of the system are found within the cluster of some ten schools that make up the village's education and schools resources. Teachers live outside the community; parents are often absent, working in the mines of Lichtenburg or the homes of Mafikeng or Johannesburg as domestics; streets are not graded, facilities are poor or often shocking in their neglect; and school results are poor.

I remember sitting through a meeting with one school. In the corner, a SADTU official sat hunched in his tracksuit, union cap defining his attitude. Towards the end of the discussion, he put up his hand. How, he asked, can one be sure that the children get a chance to see the world outside? Is it possible to set some money aside to ensure travel and trips for learners so they can experience a world beyond their village? Where we thought his union tracksuit suggested he would speak only militant rhetoric, his remarks were all about improving the prospects and opportunities for his children. How wrong first impressions can be, and how dangerous prejudices and assumptions turn out. There is clearly goodwill and energy on which to build.

Yet Bodibe as a village is extremely dysfunctional, ridden with rivalries and splits, subject to all sorts of power dynamics impenetrable by outsiders. For example, the village elders tried to gatecrash a course to which principals were taken at Wits. It had to be explained that the course was for educationists and that the hotel accommodation and meals were not perks, but essential for attendance at the course. Similarly, battles with employers about mining rights and obligations threatened to be at the expense of the processes of school building.

The Lafarge Mine, as a larger source of employment, has been a continuous factor over the years and seems to ensure at least a modicum of money in the community. Children do not appear as visibly subject to diseases of malnutrition with obvious skin welts or discoloured hair, as in villages with access only to grant monies. The potential, immediate needs and possibilities vary from school to school but there is a supporting partner to hand.

What the Trust is doing is nothing remarkable and there is no guarantee of success. Starting in 2009, it is putting R25 million into the schools over five years. Its partner in delivery is the Shanduka Foundation's Adopt-a-school project, funded by leading black businessman and ANC executive member, Cyril Ramaphosa. Expenditure and buildings are seen as a way to build commitments and participation within a school.

While much of the initial emphasis will be on the physical infrastructure, this will be tied to plans by the school and its various stakeholders, and its willingness to come on board in an enthusiastic way. The Scouts have been brought into the village with their specific programme of environmental camps for learners. The principals are being sent to participate in the Wits executive management course, alongside the district official responsible for development in the schools. The political leadership and departmental head in the province have made commitments and allocated officials to add to and support the initiatives.

The programme was launched at a sports day organised with John Perlman's Dreamfields initiative. All the players, girls and boys, received brand-new football kits in their chosen team colours, as well as equipment and tog bags. There are small gains in just getting a successful event off the ground in the face of the micro-politics. Trainers from the university in Mafikeng see the possibility of ongoing coaching, utilising the excitement of the 2010 World Cup to enhance school sports. The Trust has accelerated its credibility by actually keeping its promises – no small feat in a village that has been disappointed all too often over the years.

The different sectors in the community have found an outlet for positive and constructive contributions and perhaps begun to work together. Thus, too, corporate social investment is increasingly taking this form of focussing on a cluster of schools with a range of support programmes for a consistent and long period.

One of the other gains, of course, has been internal to Lafarge itself as a company, where mine and administrative officials have been released to encourage and motivate for this sort of community engagement. It is miles away from where such corporates used to be and how they would operate in the context of their local communities, for whom they increasingly need to take on some sort of responsibility.

This is the kind of model I have referred to – a long-term commitment, a series of measures at a number of different levels (management, teaching skills, extra-mural, infrastructure and resources), a commitment to align with departmental strategies, and a willingness to work in the most desperate of communities.

Education can be a rallying point not just for educational achievement, but hopefully for the empowerment of parents as they see the benefits that can be brought to their own children through education. It will be hard going. There is no guaranteed likelihood of success. If the initiatives can work in a bruised and dispersed environment like Bodibe, they can work anywhere. We have to keep trying, and the energy and innovation of organisations that want to contribute have to be harnessed in a strategic way.

Role models give back

There are other examples of making a hands-on long-term commitment. One of these is a movement that has become known as 'ploughback'. It involves the graduates of struggling schools making their way back to the schools that helped produce them and seeing how they can make a difference.

Even the most dysfunctional school has some children who have made it through perseverance and application. There is a layer of clerks, radio announcers, civil servants, business people and entrepreneurs, the new black middle class that has to some degree 'made it'. At the least, what they can offer to pupils at their former schools is the same kind of networks that enrich the lives of many white pupils and help them get ahead. They can create some reference point for disadvantaged kids, some point to seek help or to act as an anchor in making decisions about what is possible in life and how to go about achieving it, especially in terms of what might be required educationally speaking.

Then again, by engaging in plough-back in an organised way, it becomes more than an individual contribution made out of nostalgia. Attention is paid to a school and there is a focus from middle-class elements with some ideas of their own. This might come across as interference in the workings of a school and be resented; it might also bring resources and human capital into play that can make a difference.

My wife does this with her former school, Bridgetown High, on the Cape Flats. She and her colleagues who graduated from Bridgetown have connected with the headmaster and teachers to try to address some of their concerns. They have decided to focus on the matric years initially and take the matrics on an educational camp in which they also participate.

They can explain to the children that they are living examples of success, yet they come from exactly the same circumstances as many of the children today. In my wife's case, her parents were working class, had low earnings, her father was an alcoholic and her one sister had to work in a factory to subsidise the schooling of other family members. The stories of pain and the role models of success can only inspire today's children. Many of the graduates now doing plough-back have become teachers at other schools and so are even better prepared to intervene in educationally sound ways and to probe the possibilities.

Another fascinating example of plough-back is the bursaries that members of the Proudly Manenberg Campaign offer to working-class children in the ghettoes where they were activists and from which they have come.

A third example is the Restoration of Historic Schools Project under Archbishop Winston Njongonkulu Ndungane. Seeking to revive a tradition of excellence and achievement that existed in black education, this project has decided to focus on the many former church schools that have fallen into disrepair. Schools like Healdtown, Lemana and Tigerkloof will be rebuilt, including their physical and human infrastructure and capabilities. But of direct relevance here, one of the strategies has been to enlist the old boys and girls who went to these schools and involve them in finding solutions and identifying with their alma maters.

This movement has gone beyond the schools directly involved in the project and is beginning to see a widespread enthusiasm for this very tailor-made response. It taps into people's own sense of how schooling has helped them overcome so many obstacles in their paths to success. It has increased their determination to make a difference to the scholars who have come after them but may still sit in the same desks and use facilities that they used themselves.

Another example of this kind of applied backyard work is a lovely NGO called the Enlighten Education Trust, which operates in the Overstrand region of the Western Cape. Based in Hermanus, adjacent to the largely coloured Mount Pleasant and largely African Zwelihle townships, its new building has a music room, pottery studio, training room for educators and vocational skills, and a business advice centre and counselling room, as well as offices for the NGO workers.

Lois Kleyn is the coordinator of the NGO, and its primary work is in a range of support capacities in the ten plus schools. This includes literacy, mathematics, primary science and senior science, as well as visual arts and music. There is also pottery and dance. It brings in a range of service providers, from Ort-Tech Institute that helps with technology, to the Overstrand Training Institute that helps with youth job skills such as painting and hospitality. Enlighten Trust ensures that all schools are involved in the Junior Town Council. Teachers have been helped to do their Advanced Certificate in Education (ACE) courses, both by being encouraged to register and provided with support and mentorship. I could go on.

What we see is empathetic and expert professional assistance, good homework, research and preparation to understand the key problems and best interventions. Then there is the drawing in of a fine team and other providers who might be able to assist. Enlighten Education Trust is only five years old but has already achieved much. Its strength is the focus on a concentrated area, on a cluster of schools in its own back yard. It has also engaged in creative initiatives to find other individuals and NGOs that can help draw down the range of skills that are available in the education terrain. It lists more than 55 sponsors and supporters in its annual report for 2007/8.

It wants and expects the best for the rural children who are normally marginalised on the fringe of high-end tourist resorts like Hermanus. As Enlighten puts it in that annual report, 'Today's children will need to imagine and be innovative, abilities necessary in a global economy driven by creative problem-solving, flexible thinking and entrepreneurship.'[112]

Creative fundraising on the solid base of education programmes has become possible, as we saw with Mr Moloto in Limpopo. As Enlighten says, having its own building puts a whole different spin on things. 'For the first time we have a base from which to operate . . . we are now able to turn our dreams of a Language Laboratory, an Early Childhood Resource Centre, a reference library into reality – in fact, the sky is the limit.'[113]

Working in their back yards, not trying to change the whole world but also not being ignorant of the priorities in the wider world, it may be possible through little but comprehensive attempts like these projects, to begin to add up to a large difference that will eventually have an impact on a grand scale.

A sea change: together we can do more

No one can claim that we know exactly what will make a difference and what will work at a broad systemic level. But we have to make a start – if not a new beginning, a beginning with new elements. We cannot have more of the same and a slow, incremental approach to bringing about educational change while generation after generation of young children are cast aside.

There are many things about education that could still be said. How can a school become a centre for the community, caring for AIDS orphans, providing recreation and social space, stimulating sports? Beyond the many burdens of teaching and learning, are there ways that the school can play a part in the revival of communities and creation of a better life for all? What about early childhood development and its potential to improve the chances and prospects of children from the start? What about the way we treat our disabled and those with special learning difficulties: will we truly develop a strategy and find the money to make a difference to those among us who are most vulnerable?

These are not unimportant questions. The answers reflect on the type of society we are building, the bonds and networks of solidarity and caring we develop, the quality of our communities and our lives. Yet I have argued in this book that we need to fix the core. This does not mean that a wider set of questions is irrelevant. Still, we need to set our priorities and decide what it is that we can fix, and what we will fix first.

None of these things can be fixed quickly, or now, at once. It is hard to say this. The task is urgent; we are literally losing lives if we wait. But we have waited so long, we must move fast at the same time as we must move right. Much as we would like it to be so, there is no magic bullet that will miraculously make all else fall into place.

We have to address the three areas of influence that we know have an impact on all schools. It is all the ingredients of the toxic mix that need to be drawn out. In school, around the school, in the wider community, we need to act strategically at all three levels simultaneously. It is going to be a delicate balancing act, to get focus and impact at the same time as making sure that enough is being addressed to get a critical mass of change.

There are interim solutions, and in choosing these we need to understand that they can patch up for a short while only. For example, we do not have enough inspired and knowledgeable, dedicated and committed mathematics teachers to staff all our schools. We will not create the next generation of numerate and mathematically minded children without enough teachers. Even if we had enough for all the Grade 1 entrants now, would we have the extent and depth for the next year in Grade 2? And so on through the system? Most of these graduates from school, the new highly trained corps, would surely want to use their newly acquired skills to be accountants, engineers and business people rather than to return to school as maths teachers.

No amount of wishing is going to overcome this deficit, for which we can only blame the past. Even if we imported Indian or Zimbabwean teachers to patch some gaps (and how many would there really be?), there would still be problems. The Zimbabweans would return home if a unity government brought the progress expected in their homeland, and the Indians would still need to be housed in rural areas and learn the language. In neither case would bureaucracies in the provinces necessarily be very good at accommodating them.

The range of problems is quite deep-seated. It is not so much 'how do we fix these things?' as 'what can we do over five years, over ten years, over the next 30 years, when we think we will finally get it right?'

Fixing schools will be the work of a generation – if we start now and do it right. To even begin to deal with these things we need a plan. We need to know where we are going. We need to agree on what we want to do. It cannot be all things at once. So what are the priorities? Where will we start and how will we move?

Some of the priorities are suggested in the Education Roadmap (see Chapter 6). Improving the quality of teachers, helping teachers teach well, is the most urgent task. More than anything else, what happens at the coalface of interaction between teacher and pupil is the key. This means a whole package of attempts to enthuse, support, train and renew, and to encourage a new teaching corps, as well as to establish non-negotiables on agreed and acceptable behaviours.

The other key is to fix the departments and make sure the officials do what they are supposed to do. If this is a developmental state, the officials will have to deliver as they should. They must administer, support and provision a system so that it functions smoothly, so teachers and schools can get on with their primary task of teaching and learning. Focus needs to be placed on the districts where a school-level network of support can be built.

There is also the question of joined-up government, one of the hardest things for any state to do. How does one get the police, the sports department, culture, welfare, health, local government, all on board? More crucially, how does one get a standardised and deep-seated effort but at the same time creative application to the specifics of individual situations? One-size-fits-all does not work in education support and change. Districts need to know exactly where each school is and be able to respond to its particular problems, challenges and needs. Easier said than done.

What we need are officials like Dr Brian Wilson, a district curriculum leader based in Worcester in the Cape Winelands and working in nearby rural towns of the Little Karoo. He speaks of creating 'exceptional schools' as his task and does not understand mediocrity. He sees the aspects of support inherent in his job as multifaceted and demanding. He argues that he must pay attention to the whole cycle of learning, teaching and assessment; continuous professional development of teachers; working with the special requirements of HoDs, subject leaders and subject heads; building the School Management Teams – especially with plans around timetabling and resources; a host of administrative and financial supports to schools; and involvement and planning with the greater school community.[114]

In identifying these tasks he is immensely practical but also very focused on the pedagogical and teaching needs. His critique of the past, or what he sees as old ways of doing things that still predominate, is very clear and harsh. He argues that decisions were generally made at head office and rolled out from the top down, on the basis of perceived needs and with a one-size-fits-all approach. There was a misplaced 'cascading model' used in putting training and support in place, usually with an emphasis on outside and strict monitoring and evaluation instead of direct support. All resource-based decisions were made at head office and therefore generally not adjusted or even relevant to immediate local needs.

Against this, he works on a model that is decentralised and divides districts into manageable circuits, especially important given the geographical spread of the rural schools he must serve. He also encourages officials to really know the schools in their purview. His system builds circuit teams so that joint work is possible and gaps can be minimised. It builds responsibility and accountability in an autonomous and dynamic way, and develops a multifunctional approach that can call in specific professional assistance as needed. Finally, it puts primary focus on chalkboard support, which is both the most difficult but also the most necessary.[115]

Not all district officials can be as articulate or as clear as Dr Wilson. His experience goes back years, and his commitment to education and to the children in the front line is evident. His approach is professional and skilled, but driven. He shows that it can be done.

Teachers and the administration are the two most fundamental areas of work. Improvements in education will require tremendous focused energy and will. Bold leadership is essential. Once we have listened to all the stakeholders, conclusions will have to be drawn, paths decided, priorities fixed and resources identified to move steadily towards the goals. This will require extraordinary leadership, firstly from the education minister, then from all the MECs in the provinces. This leadership will have to be bold because many options that are not working will have to be dropped or pruned.

Can the minister be brave enough to challenge the legacy of the past and make fundamentally new demands? Will she be determined enough to demand high standards from officials and teachers, but hands-on enough to work out and adapt solutions to individualised needs and challenges? Will she listen, and will she also take decisive direction based on the inputs when this is required?

As the OECD argues in a sober but challenging way:

> Gaps exist in all countries between policy aspirations and their full implementation. In the case of South Africa, in the context of the compressed time-span, the inadequate financial resources available in relation to the nation-building processes afoot, and the fact that major educational reform is a long-term, rather than a 'quick-fix' process, what is surprising is that so much has

already been achieved, rather than that serious shortcomings continue to exist. South Africa is still in the process of transition. It will take time, sustained strategic planning and resourcing, and a steady nerve by policy makers to ensure that the reform vision is realised.[116]

To ensure that children can go back to the basics of reading and of numeracy, there needs to be a determination to put the pedagogical and learning supports in place. The education department's Foundations for Learning Campaign is a good start at equipping teachers; it is practical and focused and puts very specific demands about reading aloud and writing on the teachers and pupils.

The poorest schools need to be the focus. The goal is to focus on the dysfunctional schools, reorient them and turn them into centres of excellence, so that all children have the opportunity to learn and get ahead. The spotlight should be on mostly black primary schools in the townships and rural areas, with a focus on the poor. Here is where the lives of the vast majority need to be fixed.

This also means that the unavoidable questions of backlogs and physical resources will have to be faced. While throwing money at a problem does not in itself help, the state of many of the schools is neither encouraging nor does it build dignity and respect. All schools deserve a library and a lab, a staff room, adequate classrooms and toilets, internet and computer access, sports fields for different sports. These are simply basics for adequate learning. They will cost a lot. As a nation, South Africa will have to make a plan to find the money somehow, because resources and backlogs cannot always be hidden below the surface as questions seldom asked.

Focusing on some areas does not mean we should exclude other areas. So middle-class suburban schools should not be threatened or their stability be put at risk. Rather, as I suggested in Chapter 5, they need to become part of the solution in a more conscious and participative way. Inclusion in this way, in the overall national project of improving our schools, will in fact enhance the ability to deal with the problems in the poorer schools. The wider the mobilisation, the clearer the focus, the more that can be achieved for all.

Inclusion means there is greater room to accommodate a range of needs and strengths, not the dilution of one's goals. Diversity and difference can be strengths harnessed around a common set of concerns, a framework rather than a set of directives, a broad charter within which constituents can themselves work out how they will contribute and intervene.

There is enormous talent, professional skill and a strong will out there to fix our schools. To achieve these goals, to agree this focus, to harness all the skills, an all-inclusive process of debate and discussion is going to be needed. It will have to be coordinated and driven. It will have to be open and inclusive. Organisation and planning will undoubtedly be needed, but it must be wise enough to let initiative determine the precise outcomes. Government is not structured to 'let go' in this way, so it will have to be encouraged to acknowledge and energise a wider education constituency.

I think it is quite likely that government will have to be the driver of such a process, though it needs to animate civil society and citizens if it is to succeed. For that reason, while government must drive and resource the process, the search for solutions and their implementation cannot be entirely located within government and its structures. And it cannot be owned by government alone.

There is undoubtedly a need for a process that draws together interested parties in the widest possible way. This process is partly to deal with the politics of the education endeavour, or more correctly the micro-politics. The process is to heighten the sense of education as a social priority, as something for which the whole society will have to accept responsibility. Not government alone, but every person and every institution is going to have to put shoulder to the wheel. The weight of the past and the mistakes of the present are too heavy to be shifted without a general effort by all.

If I were the new education minister, I would do three things. The first would be a 'listening campaign' among the teachers. I would go out, from school to school, in halls and staff rooms, and hear what is bugging teachers and what they think can be done. I would give teachers the space to speak, and challenge them to search for solutions without fixating on the constraints. Teachers spend too much time in 'victim' mode, bemoaning their unfortunate circumstances.

Out of this suggested listening process would surely come key themes and a set of real, workable solutions. The relations that would be built would be valuable in getting the teachers on board with the process of education recovery, as active agents whose contribution is essential.

The second thing I would do is to begin to prepare for an all-in summit. I agree that summits in themselves do not often achieve any major goals, so it would have to be carefully prepared. The summit must be a culmination of a long and detailed process of working from the ground, of moving up to encourage the widest possible discussion, agreement and mobilisation.

In short, a mighty movement around education would have to be built at district, provincial and then national level, including all those who think they can help to put things right. This could be helped by the kind of education committees the ANC has spoken about building at community levels, as long as this is not an excuse to consolidate the power of organised but narrow stakeholders only aligned to the ANC. Similarly, the Roadmap talks about formal agreement among stakeholders to draw up a formal social compact. This kind of structured process must enhance and underscore the release of popular energy and voice. It must be open and inclusive. Thus, the parameters and the priorities and the focus will be developed in a joint and inclusive way. While of course the product is the culmination of serious listening and inclusion, it need not be totally spontaneous.

The basics of the Education Roadmap's ten-point programme would be a good starting point because it gives us all something to get our teeth into and allows for a common discussion. It is not the final word, but it prevents people from being all over the place. Obviously, suggesting the ten points as a beginning would not foreclose other areas and priorities being agreed, added or removed.

The third thing I would do if I were education minister is to have an Education Charter drawn up. This should be done in the process of the tasks I have just suggested, not as a completely separate stand-alone. An Education Charter was always an aim of the democratic movement, never realised.

Now is the time to define the non-negotiables, to say what is expected of teachers, principals, officials, the pupils themselves. How do we achieve this commitment to quality and excellence and how do we work towards it, knowing it cannot be built in a day? What are our priorities and what is our plan? Can we turn it into a set of targets and a timeframe, so we know where we should be when?

An Education Charter would define a framework within which the work of all could be enhanced. It is not that a set of priorities rules out innovation and testing or the development of niche areas of expertise. It is that it gives coherence and a thrust, within which people can better assess the kind of contribution they can make and how best to achieve that. The aim of a plan is not to constrain but to release the energy of organisations and institutions, individuals and communities.

The tasks of change are not easy and they are not quick. Steely determination and the widest possible involvement will be required. All of us will have to get on board and do our bit. As the OECD argues (and the OECD as a region, incidentally, is a stark example of the difficulties of raising output standards):

> It is clear that vision, idealism and high-minded concern for a greatly reformed education system were very much in evidence among legislators and policy makers in the early years. However, it is also clear that there was an underestimation of the time, resources and qualitative teaching force required to make operational the policy aspirations in the schoolrooms throughout the country. Much research has indicated how difficult and complex it is to achieve major educational change, even in countries where the circumstances are much more favourable than they were in South Africa. Legislation and regulation could not ensure the trans-

formation of education that was required. Experience has shown that sustained, multifaceted resourcing and supportive action are also required and the timescale for the transformation is much longer than was initially anticipated.[117]

We need a huge change in mind-set accompanied by a massive effort to improve the quality of education, especially in the poorer schools where the majority of the disadvantaged languish. There is space to debate and then to decide, and to make the moves that will help us to focus on quality education. Education has to be a highest political priority, not just of the education minister but of coordinated government. Education will have to be the responsibility of the entire country if we are to get it right.

We have to get it right and fix our schools. For our future's sake and the sake of all our children.

Endnotes

CHAPTER 1

1   UNESCO, 2004, p226.

2   UNESCO, 2004, p226.

3   ANC 52nd National Conference 2007 Resolutions, http://www.anc.org.za/ancdocs/
    history/conf/conference52/resolutions-f.html.

4   Ramphele, M, 2008.

CHAPTER 2

5   This is regarded as a derogatory term but was common in colonial parlance of the
    time.

6   *The Christian Express*, Lovedale 1878, quoted by Molteno, F, in Kallaway, p60.

7   Molteno, in Kallaway, p55.

8   quoted by Molteno, in Kallaway, p52–3.

9   quoted by Molteno, in Kallaway, p73.

10 Molteno, in Kallaway, p61.

11 Molteno, in Kallaway, p87.

12 Bird, A, in Kallaway, p194.

13 Eddie Roux, quoted by Bird, in Kallaway, p196.

14 Coplan, A, in Marks and Rathbone, p369.

15 See Edgar, R, in Kallaway, which informs the discussion that follows.

16 Edgar, in Kallaway, p185.

17 quoted by Edgar, in Kallaway, p186.

18 Edgar, in Kallaway p188–9.

19 Seekings, J and Nattrass, N, 2006, p104–5, p133–4.

20 Molteno, in Kallaway, p69.

21 Christie, P and Collins, C, in Kallaway, p166.

22 Dr Verwoerd, addressing parliament on 17 September 1953, quoted by http://www.
    statssa.gov.za/maths4stats/about.asp.

23 SACHED, p116.

24 Seekings and Nattrass, p104–5.

25 Lodge, T, in Kallaway, p328.

26 Lodge, in Kallaway, p339.

27 Truth and Reconciliation Commission (TRC) Report, p251.

28 TRC, p261.

29 TRC, p268.

30 Bloch, G, 1987, p119–20.

31 University of the Western Cape, p24–5.

CHAPTER 3

32 I use a number of shortcuts throughout the book, to try and capture the heritage of the apartheid past. These terms are always inconclusive and cannot capture the complexity of the many demographic and racial changes there have been. Sometimes the terms appear confusing. For example, 'rural' refers to farm schools and rural townships, but not the so-called 'platteland' ex-model-C schools. When I talk about 'township' schools here, it is a shorthand for the black – especially African and coloured – schools that reflect the poorer end of the spectrum and are based in the old black Group Areas and separate urban settlements, including the so-called squatter camps or informal settlements. Such terms are impossible to avoid and should be viewed with some flexibility.

33 'SA's degrees of separation' in the *Cape Times*, 27 April 2009.

34 All these measures use international standardised tests, sometimes adjusted for local language or cultural conditions. They are generally accepted as indicating a good comparative baseline of achievement across schooling systems – though again, they are symbolic and limited proxies for success. Taken together, they are so consistent they clearly show the trend to absolute mediocrity in South African school achievement relative to other countries and even local standards.

35 The test figures are usefully summarised in Fleisch, B, p4–22, and OECD, p53–5.

36 Fleisch, p8.

37 This and all other percentages in this chapter have been rounded up or down to the nearest whole number, for ease of reading.

38 Soudien, C, p61.

39 Fleisch, p8 and p10.

40 Fleisch, p13.

41 www.sacmeq.org, Fleisch p14–9, see also Van der Berg, S and Louw, M, in Bloch, Chisholm et al. (eds), p57–9.

42 Fleisch, p22.

43 Fleisch, p22.

44 Fleisch, p24.

45 Education Roadmap Diagnostics, p2.

46 Taylor, N, IJR 2006, p65–6.

47 Education Roadmap Diagnostics, p3.

48 Education Roadmap Diagnostics, p3–4. See also Louw, M, Van der Berg, S and Yu, D, p75–6.

49 Soudien, p60.

50 SAIRR 2009, p1.

51 Taylor in *Business Day*, 2006.

52 Motala, S and Pampallis, J, p61–2.

53 Allais, SM, p30.

54 OECD, p31–4.

55 Morrow, S, Panday, S and Richter, L, 2005, http://www.hsrc.ac.za/Document-395. phtml; Nelson Mandela Foundation, 2005, Ch 1.

56 Education Roadmap Diagnostics, p6.

57 http://www.sahrc.org.za.

58 Development Bank of SA, Roadmap slide 37.

59 OECD, p155–6.

60 Development Bank of SA, 2008, p187–8.

61 OECD, p373.

62 Letseka, M and Maile, S, p2–7, at www.hsrc.ac.za/document-2717.phtml; CHE, p277–8.

63 OECD, p70.

64 Letseka, M and Maile, S, p3, 5–6, at www.hsrc.ac.za/document-2717.phtml.

65 Letseka, M and Maile, S, p2–3, at www.hsrc.ac.za/document-2717.

CHAPTER 4

66 See Carnoy, M, in Bloch, Chisholm et al. (eds), p26–7 and 36–8.

67 http://p10.opennetworks.co.za/sairr.org.za/press-office/archive/news_item.2009-01-29. 1879774408 and http://www.thetimes.co.za/PrintEdition/Article.aspx?id = 823624.

68 Chisholm, L, Hoadley, U et al., p21.

69 This and all other percentages in this chapter have been rounded up or down to the nearest whole number, for ease of reading.

70 OECD, p299.

71 http://www.africancrisis.co.za/Article.php?ID = 46323 and 'Sadtu unhappy with plan to name and shame sex offender teachers', SABC, 16 April 2009.

72 'Teachers union ready to "declare war" over unpaid meetings', *Business Day*, 28 June 2008.

73 'Teachers union ready to "declare war" over unpaid meetings, *Business Day*, 28 June 2008 and 'Union hesitant about officials threat', *Business Day*, 9 June 2008.

74 'Schools not stable until Zuma is president', *Business Day*, 23 January 2009.

75 'Fight for right to meet and not teach', *Mail and Guardian*, 3 March 2009.

76 ANC 2009 Election Manifesto, policy framework, at http://www.anc.org.za/show.
    php?doc = elections/2009/manifesto/policy_framework.html&title = 2009 + Election
    + Manifesto.

77 'Teacher unions join in education campaign', *Business Day*, 10 October 2008 and
    http://www.polity.org.za/article/anc-will-transfrom-education-system---zuma-
    2009-02-27.

78 Taylor in *Business Day*, 2006, and OECD, p20.

79 Letter, *Business Day*, 2 April 2009.

80 Jansen, J, 2002, p201–2.

81 'Without honest appraisal, SA will struggle to find right place', *Business Day*, 9 Feb-
    ruary 2009 and http://www.anc.org.za/show.php?doc = elections/2009/manifesto/
    policy_framework.html&title = 2009 + Election + Manifesto.

82 OECD, p75–6.

83 OECD, p146.

84 OECD, p56.

85 Motala, Vally and Modiba, in Chisholm, Motala and Vally (eds), p 587.

86 OECD, p56.

87 Crouch, L and Patel, F, in Bloch et al. (eds), p76.

88 OECD, p41–3.

89 OECD, p42; DoE 2005, 2008.

90 56 810 candidates had incomplete results due to unmarked scripts and other failures
    in administration.

91 DoE 2008, p28; OECD, p56; 'Pandor promises all results by month-end', *Business
    Day*, 13 January 2009.

92 DoE 2008, p27.

93 OECD p57; Taylor, N, 'Raise the standards when examining matric results', *Business
    Day*, 28 January 2009; Blaine, S, 'When knowledge does not add up', *Business Day*,
    11 February 2007.

94 SAIRR *South Africa Survey 2007/8*, p341; OECD, p20; Education Roadmap Diagnos-
    tics, p10.

95 Bloch, G, 2007 and 2008, p5; DoE 2005; OECD, p341–2.

96 See Letseka, M and Maile, S, p3, 5–6, at www.hsrc.ac.za/document-2717.phtml; http://
    www.uct.ac.za/usr/ipd/dept/escan/Session%206%20Quality%20of%20Grads%20
    I%20Scott.pdf; http://www.che.ac.za/documents/d000155/index.php; and for FET
    vocational schools see 'Failure bedevils state skills schools', *Business Day* 7 July 2008.

CHAPTER 5

97 Both quotes in this paragraph are from an award application to the Impumelelo In-
    novation Awards Trust, quoted by Bloch, G, in *Focus* 41, p14.

98 Award application to the Impumelelo Innovation Awards Trust, quoted by Bloch in
    Focus 41, p14.

99 Bloch, in *Focus* 41, p14.

100 Presentation at 'Why schools work' Development Dialogue at DBSA, 27 March 2009.

101 Presentation at 'Why schools work' Development Dialogue at DBSA, 27 March 2009.

102 Christie, P, Butler, D and Potterton, M, *Report to the Minister of Education: Ministerial Committee: Schools That Work*, October 2007.

103 Christie, P, Butler, D and Potterton, M, p104.

104 Generaal Smuts Hoërskool, Vereeniging, Yearbook 2008, p2.

105 Generaal Smuts Hoërskool, Vereeniging, Yearbook 2008, p5.

106 Conversation with the author, 27 April 2009.

107 Conversation with the author, 27 April 2009.

CHAPTER 6

108 Both quotes in this paragraph are from the ANC 52nd National Conference 2007 Resolutions, http://www.anc.org.za/ancdocs/history/conf/conference52/resolutions-f.html.

109 Bloch, G. 2007, p14-5.

110 Education Roadmap, http://www.dbsa.org/Research/Documents/education_10%20 point%20plan_131108.pdf.

CHAPTER 7

111 Volkswagen 'adopts' Dinaledi school, 14 January 2009: http://www.southafrica.info/ about/education/vwdinaledi-140109.htm; for 2009/10 plans and assessment see http:// www.thutong.doe.gov.za/ResourceFiles/38643/36031/36005/2009%20financial%20 year%20Plans%20for%20Support%20of%20Dinaledi%20schools.pdf.

112 quoting US educator Stephanie Perrin, in Enlighten Education Trust Annual Report 2007/8, p10.

113 Enlighten Education Trust Annual Report 2007/8, p22.

114 Presentation at 'Why schools work' Development Dialogue at DBSA, 27 March 2009.

115 Presentation at 'Why schools work' Development Dialogue at DBSA, 27 March 2009.

116 OECD, p367–8.

117 OECD, p127.

Bibliography

Allais, SM (2009). *Quality Assurance in Education.* Johannesburg: CEPD.

Bloch, G (1988). 'Organisation as education: the struggle in Western Cape schools 1986-88' in Abrahams, S (ed), *Education in the Eighties: Proceedings of the Kenton Education Conference 1988.* Cape Town: UCT/Kenton.

Bloch, G (2005). 'Developing education in a development bank: considerations and reflections', paper to Kenton Education Conference, Mpekweni.

Bloch, G (2006). 'Education isn't just education: non-education expenditure to improve quality education', paper to CCEM Conference, Cape Town, December 2006.

Bloch, G (2006). 'State of education: lights flashing red', *Focus* 41. Johannesburg: Helen Suzman Foundation.

Bloch, G (2007 and 2008). 'The persistence of inequality in education: policy and implementation priorities', paper to DBSA Knowledge Week November 2007, and EASA Conference, Club Mykonos, January 2008.

Bloch, G (2007). 'The difficulties of systems change', paper to KMA Conference, Nairobi.

Bloch, G, Chisholm, L, Fleisch, B and Mabizela, M (eds) (2008). *Investment Choices for South African Education.* Johannesburg: Wits University Press.

Carnoy, M (2008). 'Lessons from the past two decades: investment choices for education and growth' in Bloch, G, Chisholm, L, Fleisch, B and Mabizela, M (eds), *Investment Choices for South African Education.* Johannesburg: Wits University Press.

Chisholm, L (2003). 'The state of curriculum reform in South Africa: the issue of Curriculum 2005' in Daniel, J, Habib, A and Southall, R (eds), *State of the Nation: South Africa 2003–2004.* Cape Town: HSRC.

Chisholm, L (2005) 'The state of South Africa's schools' in Daniel, J, Southall, R and Lutchman, J (eds), *State of the Nation: South Africa 2004-2005.* Cape Town: HSRC.

Chisholm, L (ed) (2004). *Changing Class: Education and Social Change in Post-Apartheid South Africa.* Cape Town: HSRC.

Chisholm, L, Hoadley,U et al. (2005). *Educator Workload in South Africa.* Pretoria: HSRC.

Chisholm, L, Motala, S and Vally, S (eds) (2003). *South Africa: Education Policy Review.* Sandown: Heinemann.

Christie, P, Butler, D and Potterton, M (2007). *Report to the Minister of Education: Ministerial Committee: Schools that Work.* Pretoria: DoE.

Council on Higher Education (2004). *South African Higher Education in the First Decade of Democracy*. Pretoria: CHE.

Department of Education (2005). *National Framework for Teacher Education, Report*. Pretoria: Department of Education.

Department of Education (2005). *Report of the Ministerial Committeee on Rural Education*. Pretoria: DoE.

Department of Education (2005, 2008). *Education Statistics 2003, 2006*. Pretoria: DoE.

Development Bank of Southern Africa (2008). *Infrastructure Barometer, 2008*. Midrand: DBSA.

Development Bank of Southern Africa (2009). 'Why schools work' Development Dialogue, 27 March. Unpublished proceedings, Midrand: DBSA.

Education Roadmap (2008) Midrand: DBSA (http://www.dbsa.org/Research/Documents/education_10%20point%20plan_131108.pdf).

Education Roadmap Diagnostics (2008). (Based on diagnostics by Servaas van der Berg and other identified research). Unpublished background paper, Midrand: DBSA.

Fiske, EB and Ladd, HF (2004). *Elusive Equity: Education Reform in Post-Apartheid South Africa*. Cape Town: HSRC and Brookings Institute.

Fleisch, B (2008). *Primary Education in Crisis*. Cape Town: Juta.

Human Sciences Research Council (2003). *Human Resources Development Review 2003: Education, Employment and Skills in South Africa*. Cape Town: HSRC and East Lansing: Michigan State University.

Institute for Justice and Reconciliation (2005). *Conflict and Governance: Transformation Audit*. Rondebosch: IJR.

Institute for Justice and Reconciliation (2008). *Risk and Opportunity: Transformation Audit*. Wynberg: IJR.

Jansen, J (2002). 'Political symbolism as policy craft: explaining non-reform in South African education after apartheid' in *Journal of Education Policy*, Vol 17 (2).

Jansen, J (2003). 'The state of higher education in South Africa: from massification to mergers' in Daniel, J, Habib, A and Southall, R (eds), *State of the Nation: South Africa 2003–2004*. Cape Town: HSRC.

Jansen, J (2005). 'Educationally essential: teachers, textbooks and time' in *Conflict and Governance: Transformation Audit*. Rondebosch: IJR.

Jansen, J and Taylor, N (2003). *Educational Change in South Africa 1994–2003: Case Studies in Large-Scale Education Reform*. Washington: World Bank.

Kallaway, P (ed) (1984). *Apartheid and Education*. Johannesburg: Ravan.

Kraak, André (2004). *An Overview of South African Human Resources Development*. Cape Town: HSRC.

Letseka, M and Maile, S (2008). *High University Drop-out Rates: A Threat to SA's Future*. Pretoria: HSRC Policy Brief March 2008 (www.hsrc.ac.za/document-2717.phtml).

Lodge, T (1983). *Black Politics in South Africa since 1945.* Johannesburg: Ravan.

Louw, M, Van der Berg, S and Yu, D (2006). 'Patterns of educational attainment and social mobility' in *Transformation Audit, Money and Morality.* Wynberg: IJR.

Marks, S and Rathbone, R (1982). *Industrialisation and Social Change in South Africa.* London and NY: Longman.

Molteno, F (1984). 'The historical foundations of the schooling of black South Africans' in Kallaway, P (ed), *Apartheid and Education.* Johannesburg: Ravan.

Morrow, S, Panday, S and Richter, L (2005). *Young People in South Africa in 2005: Where we're at and Where we're Going.* Johannesburg: Umsobomvu Youth Fund (http://www.hsrc.ac.za/Document-395.phtml).

Morrow, W and King, K (eds) (1998). *Vision and Reality: Changing Education and Training in South Africa.* Cape Town: UCT.

Motala, S and Pampallis, J (2005). *Governance and Finance in SA Schooling in the First Decade of Democracy.* Johannesburg: CEPD.

Nelson Mandela Foundation (2005). *Emerging Voices: A Report on Education in SA Rural Communities.* Cape Town: HSRC Press.

OECD (2008). *Reviews of National Policies for Education: South Africa.* Paris: OECD.

Ramphele, M (2008). *Laying Ghosts to Rest: Dilemmas of the Transformation in South Africa.* Cape Town: Tafelberg.

SACHED (1985). *The Right to Learn.* Braamfontein: Ravan/SACHED.

Scott, I, Yeld, N and Hendry J (2007). *Higher Education Monitor: A Case for Improving Teaching and Learning in South African Higher Education.* Pretoria: CHE (http://www.che.ac.za/documents/d000155/index.php).

Seekings, J and Nattrass, N (2006). *Class, Race and Inequality in South Africa.* Scottsville: UKZN Press.

Seekings, J and Nattrass, N (2007). 'Historical causes of contemporary inequality in South Africa', background paper to DBSA Development Report (unpublished).

Soudien, C (2005). 'Education: wrestling with legacy' in *Conflict and Governance: Transformation Audit.* Rondebosch: IJR.

South African Institute of Race Relations (2008). *South Africa Survey 2007/2008.* Johannesburg: SAIRR.

South African Institute of Race Relations (2009). *SAIRR Today: A View to 2020 – 3 April 2009.* Johannesburg: SAIRR.

South African Institute of Race Relations (2009). *SAIRR Today: A Challenge to the Department of Education – 30 January 2009.* Johannesburg: SAIRR (http://www.sairr.org.za/sairr-today/news_item.2009-01-28.7199358673/).

Steinberg, J (2004). *The Number.* Johannesburg: Jonathan Ball.

Taylor, N (2006). 'Fixing schools will take huge effort' in *Business Day*, 18 August 2006.

Taylor, N (2006). 'School reform and skills development' in *Transformation Audit, Money and Morality.* Wynberg: IJR.

Taylor, N, Muller, J and Vinjevold, P (2003). *Getting Schools Working: Research and Systemic School Reform in South Africa*. Cape Town: Pearson Education.

Truth and Reconciliation Commission (1998). *Truth and Reconciliation Commission of South Africa Report*. London: Macmillan.

UNESCO (2004). *Education For All: The Quality Imperative* (*EFA Global Monitoring Report 2005*). Paris: UNESCO.

UNESCO (2007). *Education For All by 2015: Will we make it?* Oxford: OUP.

University of the Western Cape (1987). *People's Education for Teachers*. Cape Town: UWC.

Van der Berg, S (2005). 'The schooling solution: primary school performance is the key' in *Conflict and Governance: Transformation Audit*. Rondebosch: IJR

World Bank (1995). *South Africa: Education Sector: Strategic Issues and Policy Options*. Washington: World Bank.

MEDIA

Media reports directly related to the Education Roadmap include:

'We must all invest in education roadmap to put SA on track' by Ravi Naidoo and Graeme Bloch (*Sunday Times*, 30 November 2008).

'Charting the course of SA schooling' by Graeme Bloch (*Cape Times*, 5 February 2009). Also as 'Ways to fix our school system' and 'Education roadmap's 10-point programme' by Graeme Bloch (*The Star*, 9 February 2009, *Pretoria News*, *Daily News*).

'ANC takes long look at education, training ahead of election' by Sue Blaine (*Business Day*, 4 October 2008).

'ANC may give OBE the chop – New Roadmap compiled at education Indaba' by Angelique Serrao (*The Star*, 14 November 2008).

'Outcomes-based education may be on the way out' (*Cape Times*, 14 November 2008).

'"Education Roadmap" calls to scrap OBE' (*The Argus*, 14 November 2008).

'"Padkaart" vir onderwys saai paniek' (*Beeld*, 15 November 2008).

'UGO opnuut in die spervuur' by Carien Kruger (*Rapport*, 16 November 2008).

'Onderwys-krisis' (*Rapport*, 16 November 2008).

'ANC considers major changes in schooling' by Sue Blaine (*Business Day*, 17 November 2008).

'Awaiting the outcome' (*Business Day*, 18 November 2008).

'More than just OBE is on the agenda' by Sue Blaine (*Business Day*, 19 November 2008).

'Union backs outcomes education' by Sue Blaine (*Business Day*, 24 November 2008).

'Back to basics' (*Business Day*, 27 November 2008).

'How to build a winning nation' (*Sunday Times*, 30 November 2008).

'Matric failure' (*Business Day* editorial, 7 January 2009).

'SA's degrees of separation' (*Cape Times*, 27 April 2009).

'No easy walk for Jacob Zuma' (*Business Day* editorial, 8 May 2009).

'Our schools of shame can be turned around' by Graeme Bloch (*The Star*, 18 May 2009).

Index

nutrition programmes 111, 117, 121, 128, 149, 158
Nyathi, Ronald 106–107

OBE, *see* Outcomes-based Education
OECD (Organisation for Economic Cooperation and Development) 11, 81, 84, 117–118, 171, 175
Outcomes-based Education (OBE) 68, 84, 103, 114, 115, 126

Pan Africanist Congress (PAC) 49, 51, 53, 95
Pandor, Naledi 107, 120–121, 150
Pandy, Thoraya 55
Parktown Boys 80, 112
Parktown Girls High 145, 147
People's Education 27, 54, 95
Perlman, John 163
Pieterson, Hector 48
Piet N Aphane High School 132–134
PIRLS (Progress in Reading Literacy Study) 65–66
plough-back 21, 154, 158, 164–167
Polokwane statement 20, 21, 107–108, 122, 149
poverty 75–79, 116, 123–124, 158
principals
    examples of excellent leadership 132–137
    importance of strong leadership 137–138
    management responsibilities 112
    Wits executive management course 135, 137, 138–141, 163
prison education 38
Progress in Reading Literacy Study (PIRLS) 65–66
Proudly Manenberg Campaign 165
Pupils' Awareness and Action Group (PAAG) 99

quality assurance 69–70, 70–71, 175
Quality Learning and Teaching Campaign 107, 129

Ramaphosa, Cyril 163
Ramphele, Mamphela 22
Ratanda 135

Reddam 80
Restoration of Historic Schools' Project 165–166
role models 164–166
Roux, Eddie 37

Sakhile Primary School 135–137
San people 30–31
School Improvement Plan (SIP) 139
school support
    assessment of ministers 118–123
    current failure 28, 85, 90, 91
    Education Roadmap 157
    infrastructure 73, 81–82, 128, 157, 172
    state responsibility 109–118
science skills 17, 62, 64, 66, 83, 102, 126
    see also literacy and numeracy; maths skills
Section 21 schools *see* model-C (formerly white) schools
Sector Education and Training Authority *see* SETA system
Selborne Primary 139–140
Selepe, Gladys Ramasela 135–137
SETA system 71, 85, 114–115
Shanduka Foundation 162–163
Shembe, Isiah 39
Smuts, Jan 37, 42, 44
societal support 90–91, 123–124, 149, 151, 157–158, 173
South African Council for Educators (SACE) 106, 145
South African Democratic Teachers' Union (SADTU) 54, 100, 106, 107, 154, 162
South African Institute of Race Relations (SAIRR) 67–68, 97, 98
South African Native National Congress (later ANC) 40–41
South African Qualifications Authority (SAQA) 70, 85–86, 114–115
South African Schools Act (1996) 125
South African Student Organisation (SASO) 48
South African Students' Movement (SASM) 48
South African Youth Congress (SAYCO) 52

Southern and East African Consortium for Monitoring Educational Quality (SACMEQ) 61, 64–65
Soweto SRC (SSRC) 48
Soweto Student Congress 53
Soweto uprising (1976) 48–50
statistics 61–68, 71–74, 125–128
Suid-Afrikaanse Onderwysersunie (SAOU) 99

Tambo, Oliver 46, 53
Taylor, Nick 66, 154
teachers
    see also SADTU
    impact of struggle 45, 98–100
    importance of consultation 173–174
    recommendations of Education Roadmap 156–157, 169
    responsibility for change 21–22
    situation in democracy 82–85, 100–106
    teacher training 84, 99, 101, 127, 128
    teacher unions 100, 106–109, 154
Teachers' League of SA (TLSA) 51, 99
teacher unions 100, 106–109, 154
    see also SADTU
technikons 127, 128
    see also higher education
textbooks 83, 102, 120, 156
Thibedi, TW 37
Third International Mathematics and Science Study (TIMMS) 61–62, 63–64
Tigerkloof 27, 36, 165
trade unions 37, 42, 50, 100, 106–109
traditional societies 27, 30–34, 36
Transvaal African Teachers' Association (TATA) 45
TRC (Truth and Reconciliation Commission) 52

unemployment 76–78, 124
    see also poverty
UNESCO 10, 18–19, 20, 63, 90
UNICEF 63
United Democratic Front (UDF) 51, 52, 54–55, 99
Unity Movement 45, 51
Universal Negro Improvement Association (UNIA) 39, 40
universities 52, 61, 80, 86–87, 115, 127, 134
    see also higher education
University of the Free State 80, 115
University of the North (Turfloop) 52
University of the Western Cape (UWC) 52

Van Riebeeck, Jan 33
Verwoerd, HF 43
Vilakazi-Tselane, Linda 138, 140
violence
    bullying 80, 104, 113–114
    current violence in schools 80–81
    during struggle 91–96
vocational training system 85, 115, 127

white schools see Model-C (formerly white) schools
Wilson, Dr Brian 170–171
Wits Education Policy Unit 70
Wits executive management course 135, 137, 138–141, 163
Worcester 170

Zenex Foundation 159–160
Zionist churches 39
Zuma, Jacob 20, 107, 134, 149
Zwelihle 166–167

About the author

GRAEME BLOCH is an education policy analyst at the Development Bank of Southern Africa (DBSA). He taught in the education faculty at the University of the Western Cape and was project manager for youth development at the Joint Education Trust.

He is a graduate of the University of Cape Town where he specialised in economic history. He is a member of the UCT Council, serves as director on the Lafarge Education Trust and is a judge in the Impumelelo Innovation Awards.

Bloch has worked as head of Social Development in the Department of Welfare, and as Director of Social Development in the Joburg Metro. Before 1994, he was executive member of the National Education Crisis Committee (NECC) as well as the United Democratic Front (UDF). For his involvement in the democratic movement he was detained and arrested numerous times, and he was banned from 1976–81.

He has published a number of books and articles about education.